P9-ELO-179

PARENTS
Talk With Your Children

V. GILBERT BEERS

HARVEST HOUSE PUBLISHERS
Eugene, Oregon 97402

PARENTS: TALK WITH YOUR CHILDREN

Copyright © 1988 by Harvest House Publishers
Eugene, Oregon 97402

Library of Congress Cataloging-in-Publication Data

Beers, V. Gilbert (Victor Gilbert), 1928-
    Parents, talk with your children.

    1. Parent and child—United States.   2. Parenting—
Religious aspects—Christianity.   3. Communication in
the family—United States.   I. Title.
HQ755.85.B44   1988   306.8'74   87-082257
ISBN 0-89081-597-6

To Arlie, my lovely wife,
who gave up everything
to be wife and mother,
but enjoyed it so much that she
never thought she gave up anything.

Contents

Introduction

Hindsight always seems clearer than foresight because it merely retraces steps already taken rather than anticipates the unknown future. This is a book about hindsight, a reflection concerning 35 years of parenting and that most important ingredient, talking.

Arlie and I have a confession to make: When our five children were born, we didn't have a master plan. We didn't say, "Let's do this and it will all work out that way." In a rather simplistic way we launched into parenting, enjoyed it so much that we gave our highest priorities to it, and then discovered much later how richly rewarded we were in parent-child relationships.

In the early years of parenting I would have enjoyed a book by someone who had gone that way before. I would have appreciated counsel that said, "Here are things you must do and things you must avoid." I would have enjoyed an older brother's or sister's footprints that showed the pitfalls to avoid and the right places to go.

But I would want to know that this counsel came from experience, not merely from reading. I would want to know that my counselor's children came through okay.

My children should be writing this introduction. Each of them is a Christian and each has married a Christian. Each is deeply concerned to raise his or her children in a Christian home. They came through okay.

The focus of this book is the essential ingredient in parent-child relationships: parents and children talking with each other. It all sounds so simple, and it is. But it's so simple that many parents miss this ingredient: cultivating lifelong friendships through talking. Start early. Keep it up. Do it with delight. But do it!

—V. Gilbert Beers

PARENTS
Talk With Your Children

1

Something You Absolutely MUST Have

One of our favorite family videotapes is "Sleeping Beauty," I suppose partly because it is the all-time favorite of our grandchildren and partly because it is one of the few Hollywood movies with strong Christian values. The prince dares to have a cross on his shield and dares to fight evil with good. The entire movie is the victory of good over evil, and the most significant weapon is the sword of truth.

Imagine Hollywood doing that!

A favorite scene in "Sleeping Beauty" is the emotional moment in the throne room when three very human-looking fairies (good fairies, of course) bestow their gifts upon the infant Princess Aurora.

"My gift shall be the gift of beauty," says one.

"My gift shall be the gift of song," says another. Before the third can bestow her gift, the evil Maleficent appears with her gift: The Princess Aurora will prick her finger on the spindle of a spinning wheel before her sixteenth birthday and will die.

Now the third fairy must change her intended gift, transcending Maleficent's evil prophecy of death to bestow the gift of sleep (until love's first kiss would waken her). But what was that wonderful gift which the third fairy was about to give?

Our family has often talked and wondered about that mysterious, unknown gift. Since the little princess already had the gift of beauty and the gift of song, and of course all the wealth, power, and prestige of royalty, what more did she need? I suppose it could have been an extra bonus of poise, or charm, or generosity, or fame, or adventure, or some other "extra." But those don't match the stature of the other two gifts, beauty and song. No, it had to be more valuable than a mere bonus. Perhaps the answer to this question may lie in the values associated with our own God-given gifts.

Of all the personal gifts that you have, which one do you value the most? Which one is truly indispensable, so that you could not live a rich and full life without it?

I've asked myself that question. If I had to lose all but one gift, which would I prize most of all? Which would be the last I would want to give up, the one I would relinquish most reluctantly?

The gift of sight is a prime candidate. I would not want to lose my sight. I love to see the mountains and the valleys. I love to watch the sunset and the sunrise. The majesty of the skies, with billowy clouds, great storms, and rainbows, is awesome. I could stare at the sky all day and wonder at its beauty. I love art and colors and design. I love to read. I love the beauties of flowers and trees and so many other wonderful things in God's creation. I love to watch my children and grandchildren, to watch the twinkle in their eyes as we interact. I love to look at my wife's face and see her smile. No, I would not want to lose the gift of sight.

But through the years I have had blind friends. They are some of the most sensitive people I know. Deprived of one of their five senses, they seem to compensate in the sensitivities of the mind and heart. I would not want to be blind, but I could be blind and live a rich, full life. I know I could.

What about the gift of sound, or hearing? I'm a devotee of classical music, and often listen to Mozart or Bach, Beethoven or Vivaldi, Haydn or Liszt, Handel or a hundred other great composers while I read. I love to hear a waterfall or a babbling brook or the whisper of the wind sighing in the trees. I love a summer evening with the occasional muffled "whooo" of an owl, frogs in symphony by the lakeside, or the soft lapping of water against the shore.

I love to hear voices, whispers, or even shouts. All of life is a great choir of beauty, a symphony of sound, and I would not want to miss a note of it. With the hymnwriter I sing, "This is my Father's world, and to my list'ning ears all nature sings, and round me rings the music of the spheres." I love to participate in God's joyous symphonic creation. But if I were deaf I could still enjoy a rich life of reading and seeing, touching and tasting. Others do. I know I could.

Then there is the gift of touch. You never know how important this is until you hurt deeply or lose someone precious to you, then feel a friend's arm around you or feel a loved one's warm embrace.

What would the gift of married love be without the gift of touch, the tender strength of skin against skin, the warm glow of lips that gently caress your own with a quality of fire more vibrant than any flame? Loving touch is a gift of wonder. I would not accept any amount of money to relinquish it. You wouldn't either, when you think about it. True love is a banquet table enriched with the delights of touch. But if I lost the gift of touch I could still see and hear, and I know I could enjoy a full, rich life.

Yesterday 14 of our family members sat down at our usual Sunday dinner together. The gift of scent and the gift of taste teamed up at our big family dinner to present a most wonderful duet. You don't know what scent and taste can do for you until you participate in a family dinner with homestyle cooking the way Arlie does it!

This was our granddaughter Sarah's sixth birthday, so she was queen for the day. Nobody dared to start eating dessert, a delicious homemade birthday cake, until she took her first bite. But nobody complained. It was a celebration of birthday, but it was also a continued celebration of scent and taste with the cake Arlie had lovingly made for Sarah, graced with ice cream and accented with steaming hot coffee.

What's better on a cold winter morning than the scent and taste of pancakes with maple syrup, or bacon and eggs? Remember the smell, and then the taste, of hot buttered popcorn at the zoo, or ice cream bars or hot dogs that you bought on a summer day at the ball game?

What would we do without the gifts of scent and taste? I remember that exquisite gourmet meal with friends in that only-once-every-so-often restaurant. There were sauces and savory flavors that only trained chefs know how to create. Those are special times to test our precious gifts of scent and taste to their limit. I would not want to lose either of those gifts.

I love to smell a rose or iris in the spring, the unique scent of the ocean as I walk along the shore, and fresh-baked bread when it first comes piping-hot from the oven. I hope I never lose my gifts of scent or taste. But if I did, I could still live a rich, full life with my other senses. I know I could, and I would.

The Princess Aurora already had her five senses, and because she was royalty they would be pampered to the limit, so the third fairy would not and could not have given any of these gifts. Her gift had to be something that transcends, but perhaps utilizes, these remarkable gifts.

God bestows these five precious gifts indiscriminately upon tiny infants around the world, princesses and peasants alike. So what gift could the third fairy have given? What gift was not given, but would transcend them all?

The story never tells us. So let me guess. I will guess by telling what I would have given had I been that third fairy. I would have given the gift of simple eloquence, or should I say eloquent simplicity, the gift of life-building conversation, the gift of redemptive talk.

Perhaps you are thinking, "But I *have* the gift of talk, and so did the Princess Aurora. Why waste a precious gift on something which the little princess (and I) already had?"

It's true that each of us has the gift *to* talk, but few of us develop the gift so that it is the gift *of* talk—redemptive talk, saying things that change lives, building lives with what we say.

I think each of us has a longing to talk meaningfully, purposefully, and redemptively with each other. We want to talk so that others will listen and will feel uplifted and revitalized when they do. I think we have a desire to enhance one another with our conversation, but I know of very few people who practice that gift. Why not? Why don't we do more of it? Why don't we fill our days with this kind of talk?

I think the answer is simple: neglect. Neglect because we live too close to, and take for granted too much, those with whom we can cultivate this gift daily.

We neglect the most obvious opportunity in the world to build the art of redemptive talk when we fail to cultivate the gift of redemptive communication daily with our spouse and children. There is no better place to begin than in the sanctity of our own home, with husband or wife, daughter or son.

This is a book about talking redemptively with our children. But the foundation upon which we talk redemptively with our children is talking redemptively with our husband or wife. You really cannot separate the two; they are part of the same package.

Is it possible that we are "saving up" our best talk for outsiders, for strangers? Is it possible that we have deceived ourselves into thinking that we should engage in our best talk with people who care the least about us and engage in talk that is trite with those who love us most?

If you are a parent, responsible for children, the Lord God of heaven and earth has delegated to you one of His most valuable assets: a life under construction. And He has given to you His most powerful, yet most simple, of all gifts to fulfill His mission for you.

Through the gift of talk, of conversation and communication with your child, God has endowed you with the power to change an important corner of His world. This gift utilizes each of our five basic gifts (sight, hearing, touch, taste, smell) and yet transcends them all.

In His divine wisdom God provides this remarkable gift free, yet it is infinitely valuable. It is a gift whose value is in using it rather than possessing it. Deprived of this gift, life shrivels into atrophy. Refusing to share this gift, life withers and dies. It could well have been the third fairy's gift! God thought it significant enough to give it as one of His prime gifts, so we have a hint of its enormous value.

We're talking about the gift of communication, preeminently as powerful as it is simple. Or should we call it "talk" instead of communication? Actually we need another word less formal than "communication" but more embracing than "talk." We need a word that captures the essence of the beauty and power of talk with each other that changes each other. Unfortunately, there is no such word. We are referring to more than speaking, verbalizing, vocalizing, conversing, discussing, or any of the other synonyms. Throughout this book we will use the word "talk," or sometimes "conversation" or "communication," but you'll understand that what we're trying to get across is more than any of these.

"Communicate" actually gets at the idea better than "talk," but the word is too clinical for the wondrously personal dynamic that exists between two people who are using this remarkable gift. "Conversation" portrays the personal dynamic, but can't lay hold of the wonder of it all, the redemptive, life-building quality we're talking about here.

Actually life-building talk is a gift too splendid for even a fictitious fairy. It is a gift so majestic that it could come only from the mind and heart of the Creator of the universe Himself.

No one but the Lord of Creation could conceive of a way for two people to establish a pipeline, an invisible umbilical cord, a powerline, between themselves which would transmit personhood back and forth in a two-way process. Only He could establish a system by which two people can enhance one another, yet in the process enrich self. Only the God who made heaven and earth could imagine a gift that we can bestow as a thousand little gifts, yet accumulate into one grand gift that transforms me into a new me in the process of transforming you into a new you.

What more simple, yet majestic, gift is there than the gift of talking with one another, but realizing that something very special is happening to each of us as we do it? What more enriching gift can I bestow upon you than talking with you, communicating my ideas and feelings, my heritage and emotions, my dreams and visions? More important than communicating these things *to* you is communicating *with* you in such a way that the best of each of us emerges.

You notice, I'm sure, that this book is about talking "with," not talking "to." If I merely talk *to* you, the dynamic is lost. It's a one-way street. I'm dumping myself on you but am accepting nothing back from you. That's why so many husbands and wives have communications problems; they talk *to* each other but not *with* each other. They make each other a personal dumping grounds, and nobody wants to be a personal landfill.

Could that be why so many parents and children have communications problems—they talk *to* each other but not *with* each other? They dump the dark side of self on each other and expect the other person to like it.

The gift of life-changing talk is a special gift that God reserved for His highest order of creation—people. Some animals communicate on a low plateau with each other, of course. They express anger and they bully each other. They show fear and they communicate so that they propagate and carry on their species. But their communication is nothing compared to ours.

I grew up on a farm with many animals. It was easy for a mischievous growing boy to communicate fear to animals. Walk into a chickenhouse, wave your arms and shout, and there arises a cacophony of squawks, clucking, and flying feathers.

Chickens, and other animals too, also communicate fear to one another. The king of the chickenyard strikes terror in any other rooster who infringes on his territory. But even though they communicate emotions, I have never seen two chickens, or any other animals, sit down and have a good talk about their relationships. They are content to satisfy their hunger, thirst, and biological impulses, and to rule the roost when they can. If people communicate no better than animals, they build each other (and their relationships) no better than animals.

Animals may even build elementary relationships, but what they can do is nothing compared to the relationships God permits us to build through talk, a most remarkable gift.

We humans are made in the image of God. Like God, we can build long-lasting, even eternal, relationships between two personalities—two human persons, or a human person with God. It is this dynamic link between two personhoods that points to the creative genius of God and His willingness to create people in His image. For it is in exercising this remarkable gift of communication (talk, if you please) between each other and between us and God that we reveal His image.

I think that's it! The image of God is reflected in us and from us as we enhance Godlike qualities (godliness, if you please) in one another. For that purpose we were created, and when we fulfill our created purpose we achieve ultimate happiness. We discover the joy of living as we build in one another those remarkable qualities that distinguish us as "godly," qualities such as love, joy, peace, patience, kindness, goodness, faithfulness, gentleness, and self-control (Galatians 5:22,23).

All people are granted this remarkable privilege, although few exercise it. For parents, entrusted with the care and nurture of a child, "talking with" takes on new meaning. Your child depends upon you, more than any other human, to build his or her life as God designed it to be. That's why talking with your child in a life-building way becomes the majesty of divine eloquence wrapped in the garments of childlike simplicity. Wasn't that what Jesus did?

Let's think, for example, about that Mount Everest of doctrine, the grandest theme of all, that towering mountain peak called love. There is no more awesome, panoramic, majestic concept on earth than that. We thrive or die because of love. The redemptive love of God boggles the mind, even of the most astute theologian.

The apostle Paul himself seemed to gasp in wonder as he spoke of how wide and long and high and deep is the love of Christ (Ephesians 3:18). It was as though this brilliant, learned man viewed the majesty of love as he stood on the rim of the Grand Canyon of doctrine, filled with the swirling seas of personal awe, framed by the magnificent snowcapped mountain peaks of worship, overarched with towering storm-clouds of wonder, and highlighted with the jewellike qualities of a great rainbow of promise. His reaction was a rather sophisticated way of saying, "Wow! Is this love?"

And yet this vast, unfathomable idea called love is as simple as a little child jumping onto your lap, giving you a hug and kiss, and whispering those three magic words, "I love you." The very essence of God's grandest theme is condensed into a child's whisper, soft lips on our cheek, a child's touch. Or our soft whisper in our child's ear!

We who are parents are entrusted with the incredible privilege of communicating with our smallest child about things like love, in terms of endearment and with utter simplicity.

I think I prize this gift most of all—the gift of enriching and enhancing your life, and the lives of my children, my grandchildren, and my wife by talking in a life-building way. I prize it most because it's the gift that does the most for me as well as those I touch. Redemptive talk is a two-way gift, the only one I know that builds me as I build others. I could lose sight or taste or hearing or any of my basic senses and still enjoy life. But if I lose this precious gift of life-building talk, I lose the essence of life itself. I will wither and die. But through this gift you and I can become architects and contractors and foremen and craftsmen and laborers in the eternal process of building our children's lives (and our own too) as God intended. That's worth talking about, isn't it?

In summary, here are some guidelines concerning that most important gift of communication, or talk, with our children:

1) God has granted us who are parents a unique privilege, for He has entrusted the life-building process for that important person, our child, into our care. This is a high and holy calling.

2) Our most effective means of building our children's lives is through conversation (talk), supported by role-modeling. Our communication between parent and child is a grand opportunity to be mutually constructive.

3) As parents, we should cultivate the habit of talking *with* our children rather than merely talking *to* them. Conversation, communication, talk, is a two-way street.

2

Build Up or Shut Up

Through the years we've had a little saying in our family: "Build up or shut up." It's not a very delicate way to phrase what we're trying to say, but it really does get the point across. I've asked myself what would happen to our nation if all government figures adopted our little slogan, really adopted it! The election process would change dramatically, wouldn't it? Candidates for office would have to focus on issues instead of personalities. Government figures would stop assassinating one another verbally for political purposes. Government might spend more time governing. That would be very worthwhile at any level of government, wouldn't it? From city politics to national politics, life would be much different and much more purposeful.

How about life at the office? Opportunists who want to climb the corporate ladder on the bodies and reputations of fellow workers would need to resort to hard work for advancement. Think of it: The office would change, productivity would change, and we might spend less money for a higher-quality product when we go to the store.

But it's too idealistic to think this will happen in government or the workplace. I would settle for "build up or shut up" in the Christian community and home. Perhaps that's too idealistic also, although it shouldn't be.

This book is about parents and how they talk with their children, so we will not get involved here with "build up or shut up" in the Christian community except to say that it is a biblical ideal worth working for because the Lord Himself mandated it. This is a chapter about "build up or shut up" between parents and children. Indirectly it must also involve our little slogan between parents.

I believe the two most basic questions in life are "Why am I here?" and "What should I do about it?" Happiness comes from the way we answer these two questions.

"Why am I here?" is a question about purpose. For what purpose did God put me here on earth? On the Damascus Road, rebellious, mean-spirited, murderous Saul met Jesus. When he did, his first question was "What do you want me to do?" It's another way, an action-oriented way, of asking "Why am I here?" When we understand what God wants us to do, we understand why we are here. When we understand why we are here, we understand what God wants us to do. These are intertwined, like the strands of a tightly woven rope.

Some people have struggled with "Why am I here?" under the heading of "Knowing the Will of God." That's another way of saying the same thing. When I know the will of God for me, I know why I am here and what He wants me to do. It's the same rope again, with the three questions woven as one.

I have wrestled with this interwoven question for the past 43 years since I became a Christian. I know the answer for me. You will have to discover it for yourself, of course, but may I share with you what I believe the answer is for me? It may help you determine the answer for yourself.

For me, there is one answer to "Why am I here" or "What do you want me to do, Lord?" or "How can I know the will of God?" I believe that God has answered something like this: "You are in my life-building business." Not any old life-building business, but God's. God is too gracious to say, "Build up or shut up," but I think that's the idea.

As a disciple of Christ, I am in the same business that He is in. Theologians call it redemption. We may call it life-changing or life-building. Christ's redemption involved a sacrificial death. I can't do that, but I can engage in sacrificial living. Only God's Son could die for my salvation. But my redemption for others, my life-building or life-changing, involves the way I live.

First, as a husband, God expects me to build up my wife. *Building our mate* is the primary mission of marriage—not what we can get out of our mate. If you aren't building your mate each day, it's time to ask why you got married. If your marriage is in trouble, one of the first questions to ask is "When was the last time I built up my mate?" followed by "How did I do it?" followed by "What can I do today to build my mate?" Of course this is a two-way street, and your mate is equally mandated to build you.

A friend who made no claim to be a Christian told me that he and his wife each day make a game of building the other. Each day is a new surprise, a new excitement, of something special that each does to build the other, to make the other person feel like a king or queen, to make the other person a better, stronger, happier person. I was ashamed when I heard my friend describe this. I am a Christian and he makes no claim to be one, but he is following the biblical mandate for marriage much better than I am.

Second, as a father, God expects me to build up my children (and as a grandfather, my grandchildren). The mission of parenting is not standing idly by, watching your children grow up, but serving as a construction engineer in their growing lives, for the glory of God the Architect.

Let me throw in that theological term again. God has called us as parents to live *redemptive* lives. As husbands and wives we are called to live redemptively toward our mates. As parents we are called to live redemptively toward our children.

For God's glory we are in the life-building business. He has commissioned us to build up our mates and our children. He has also commissioned us to build up members of our extended family, our neighbors, our fellow workers, and those in the church of Christ worldwide. But this book is about the parental life-building business, and the example which spousal life-building sets for growing children.

Life-building is not one compartment of parenting; it is all of parenting. Everything I do as a parent should be done as part of the life-building process. It should be redemptive.

When I discipline my children I must ask, "Is this redemptive, is this building my child's life as God wants it built?" If it isn't, I need to change the way I discipline. Discipline that merely helps me get anger off my chest is not discipling, but is merely question-able therapy for me. There are better ways for you and me to get therapy.

Most of us feel relieved at times when our children get off to school, or play at a neighbor's house, or watch TV so that we can "get our work done." What we really mean is that this gives us free time to get our chores done. Our real work as parents is guiding our children as God wants. Our chores are not our real work; our children are. Chores are necessary interruptions to our real work. We should never think of our children as interruptions to our work. They *are* our work! Building their lives is God's commissioned purpose, His will, for parents.

When my children come home from school and want to talk with me, do I view this as an interruption or as an opportunity to do some of my life-building work for God? When we sit down at breakfast or dinner, is this a time to straighten things out or build things up?

Am I more concerned with what my child doesn't do than what my child does do? Do I spend more time telling my child what he or she did wrong than I do helping my child know what to do right?

Today, each time you interact with your child, ask, "Is this building up?" If you do this, you will be surprised to see how today will be different from yesterday.

In summary, here are three guidelines for us to follow as we seek to build the lives of our children (and our mates, too):

1) We parents are in the business of life-building, building lives for the Master Architect.

2) When we work, or play, or discipline, or whatever we do as parents, we need to remember that we are doing these as a vital part of our life-building work.

3) Our children *are* our work. Our chores are the interruption to our work. We need to get our priorities in order.

3

Your Children Can Become Your Best Friends

A young minister and his wife in another city have an ever-present welcome mat out for Arlie and me. When we go for a visit (several times each year) they try to arrange their work so that we can spend the two or three days together. We go on hikes together, go to dinner together, play games together, and talk the hours away.

Their home is our home. Our home is their home. If they have to leave for a short time, they give us the key to their home and we come and go as if it were our own. Friends who drop in unexpectedly surely must see that this couple and we are "best friends." This is the kind of friendship we all dream of.

This warm, wonderful friendship will never end. I know it won't. How do I know? Because the minister's wife is our daughter Jan, and she has always been one of our best friends, since the day she was born.

We were there not long ago, and as we walked into the house I looked at Kevin and Jan and pondered this friendship. Each is a strikingly good-looking, mature Christian with a heart to serve God and a desire to

build up other people. I know you would feel privi-
leged to be their friends. We do.

As I looked at this bright, articulate couple I asked
how this friendship came to be. How is it that our role
as parents was transcended by a friendship as our
children grew into the adult years?

Arlie and I feel this same close friendship with each
of our children. When Cindy comes home from college (now with her soon-to-be husband Rob), we make
a pot of coffee or hot chocolate, and sit down to talk.
We talk about anything and everything, and it's not
uncommon to talk for an hour or more at a time. In the
winter we build a fire in the fireplace in our country
kitchen and enjoy one another's presence as we talk
away the moments together.

It's the same with Kathy and her husband Brad, or
Ron and his wife Becki. Sundays and birthdays and
holidays and special days are times to get together for
dinner and celebrations and talk. Without question,
our children are our best friends.

But why? How? When they were born we didn't
say, "We're going to become best friends with our
children." At that point the idea never even occurred
to us. We were consumed with the idea of being good
parents, not best friends.

But when each of our children was born, we thought
of that child as 1) a full, complete person, and 2) someone equal to us in God's eyes. We never viewed our
child as only part of a person, less than a person, or
someone who would emerge into personhood. Each
child was always a person, a full person, a complete
person. We began thinking that way as soon as we
knew that Arlie was pregnant. There was a person,
although an unknown person, growing in her. At
birth that person broke upon our horizon with all the

attributes of personhood. Now the child had a face, a body we could cuddle and feed, a personality, a name.

I can honestly say we never viewed our children as less than us. We always thought of them as equal to us. I believe this profoundly shapes the way we discipline our children, guide our children, talk with our children.

Of course they were smaller than we. Of course we were commissioned by God to be their guides, their disciplinarians, their shepherds, their protectors, their caretakers. We fed them, clothed them, diapered them, taught them to tie their shoes, and helped them learn a hundred other small but necessary skills. There were many times we had to say no. There were many times we had to suggest an alternative. There were times we had to spank them. Yes, there were even times when we yelled at them! I'm not sure those were always redemptive, productive times, but they reminded us that we too are human.

I think the foundations of friendship are laid over long periods of time. Friendship is something that ages well. It matures with the passing of time. It stands the test of time. Friendship that is transient is not a valued friendship.

I was struck with this idea on our most recent visit with Kevin and Jan. We had this wonderful relationship, not because we decided at some point in her teen years or postcollege years to be friends, but because we have always been friends. The foundations of our friendship were laid when Jan was born (and the same was true of our other children). We enjoyed eating together, talking together, and hiking together on our recent visit because we have always enjoyed doing these things together. I've often said that if you want your children to hike with you when they are 25, you'd better be hiking with them when they are 5. If you want them to *enjoy* hiking with you when they are 25, you'd better enjoy hiking with them when they are 5.

If your children are an interruption to you when they are 5, you will be an interruption to them when they are 25. If you are glad to get your children out of your way when they are 5, they will be glad to get you out of their way when they are 25.

Building a friendship with children is interwoven with building trust with children (isn't this true of any friendship?). Friendship is a manifestation of a relationship of trust. When trust ends, friendship ends.

Trust says, "You can count on me; I will always be there when you need me." Trust says, "What I say is what I am and what I am is what I say." Trust says, "You can count on me in tough times as much as in good times." Trust says, "I will look for the best in you, not the worst." Trust says, "I want you to succeed, not to fail." Trust says, "I will be there even when it is not in my own best interests to be there; I will be for you when others are against you; I will love you even when it appears that you hate me."

Is this why we can trust God so much? Aren't these the promises He has made to us? They are the same promises which Christian parents should make to their children. When our children realize that we are not only *making* these promises to them but are also *keeping* them, a relationship of trust develops, and a true friendship develops.

Trust is promises kept. Trust is consistency realized. Trust is seeing priorities in perspective. Trust is assurance that circumstances will not change relationships. Trust allows a measure of forgiveness for a margin of error. Trust is security, the sure knowledge that you will be the same toward me tomorrow as you are today and were yesterday. Trust watches you build me and enjoy doing it. Trust is the thread from which the tapestry of friendship is woven, the clay from which the vessel of friendship is shaped, the gold from which the ring of friendship is cast.

Parents are in the business of establishing and maintaining trust in their children, as God is in the business of establishing and maintaining our trust toward Him. God is to be trusted because He is trustworthy. Parents must gain trust the same way.

If you want to establish and maintain your child's trust in you, and thereby establish and nurture a friendship with your child, here are some basic requirements:

1) Be consistent. Develop expectations for your child and stick with them. Nothing is more confusing to a child, or us, than to have shifting standards. If you have rules, make sure they are reasonable rules, then stick with them. Of course there are margins for exceptions. There are times when rules do not fit the circumstance. You and your child must rely on your good judgment to come up with a reasonable verdict for that moment. But usually the rule does fit and you should stick with it. Consistency builds a sense of security in your child. Consistency builds parameters that help your child know how far is too far and prevents the child from having to make adult judgments before he is ready.

2) Be reasonable. Our God distinguishes Himself from pagan gods in His reasonableness. He does not ask us to lie on beds of nails or push a marble up a mountain to gain His love. He does not ask us to torture ourselves or destroy ourselves to prove our devotion. God asks us to obey, to keep our lives within His boundaries of love. We parents should have the same standard of reasonableness. If we have made a rule that doesn't work for a certain situation, we should be reasonable and say, "I expect you to keep

rules, but not when we agree that one doesn't work. Here is one time it doesn't work. Let's set a new boundary for this situation."

3) Be loving. God's mark of distinction is also love. Pagan gods were not presented as persons who loved their worshipers, certainly not enough to die for them. God is unique in that most wonderful quality. If your child knows that you love him no matter what, even when he doesn't deserve your love, it becomes more difficult not to obey. Even discipline should be done in love, not in angry vengeance.

4) Be involved. Building trust, and friendship, cannot be done at a distance. I've never met a family that is close-knit without at least one parent devoting life and love to that family. Sometimes a wife may have to compensate for a husband whose job requires constant travel. Sometimes a husband may have to compensate for a wife who has intense career goals. Some husbands and wives team up in the business of parenting, making that their primary objective in life. But without loving parental involvement, trust is not easily built. Involvement is presence, being there, being there *with* your child. There is no substitute.

5) Be *for* your child. I heard an elderly man describe his painful childhood and youth. His father was abusive and mean-spirited. He was not in the business of building his son. He was obviously not *for* his son, but made it his life's mission to treat his son harshly and to dump his mean-spiritedness on his son. Not surprisingly, the son grew up to hate the father and was relieved when his father died. The bitterness remained in the son's heart, even when he grew to be old. The story is tragic for any father and son, but doubly tragic since each claimed to be a Christian.

We parents must ask if we are truly *for* our child. Are we in the business of making our child succeed, even making our child look better than us? I believe that one of the finest goals of parenting is to build your child into a higher level of effectiveness than you were able to attain.

It is this spirit of being *for* your child that gives the child security in family and home. If a child is casting about, searching in strange places for security, it is well to ask if he is finding adequate security (*for*-ness) at home.

The spirit of this is captured in Romans 8:31: "If God is for us, who can be against us?" A child might expand this to say, "If my parents are for me, who can be against me?"

When our children went through their teen years, Arlie and I projected the message of Romans 8:38,39 into our parenting. "Nothing you can ever do will separate you from our love," we would tell our children. "If you do something you shouldn't, you may break our hearts, but you will not stop us from loving you."

In a recent interview on 100 Huntley Street (an excellent Canadian Christian television program), a lady in the audience asked what she should say to her son when children at school made fun of him because he was a Christian. My answer was this: "Be sure he has a strong and secure base at home with parents who are truly *for* him. When children have that, they can stand up against almost anything. Take that away, and how can they stand against anything?"

My trust in God is much deeper because I know that He is *for* me. My trust in my parents was also deeper because I knew they were *for* me. I believe the close friendship that Arlie and I have with our children comes largely from their assurance that we were, and are, *for* them, no matter what.

Trust is the fruit of talk—honest, sincere talk. We trust each other by communicating with each other. It is no different with our children. They learn to trust us as we communicate trust, verbally and nonverbally, through the years.

In summary, here are three important guidelines in building a lasting friendship with your children:

1) Your children will become your best friends if you establish the basis for friendship in your parenting. Watching your children become your best friends is one of the rich fruits, the true delights, of parenting.

2) Building a friendship with your children is based upon building their trust in you, and that is built largely through our conversation.

3) Building a friendship with your children is building a relationship of unquestionable trust, which is built through our consistency, reasonableness, love, involvement, and being *for* them no matter what.

4

Person to Person

Somewhere I heard about a father-to-be who spent his evenings fixing a bedroom to become the nursery and in painting, papering, getting new furniture, and helping his wife get life's little necessities in order for the soon-to-come-on-the-scene new baby.

"You're spending all your spare time getting ready for the new baby, aren't you?" a friend remarked.

"Yes," said the father. "I've never before spent so much time getting the house ready for a person I've never met."

Already in this father's and mother's mind they were thinking of their baby-to-be as an important person. And they should. A new baby is one of the most important VIP's on earth, a brand-new person who has joined the world scene and will soon leave footprints (handprints too, some with jam and peanut butter) all over it.

Walk into a room filled with dignitaries and you may barely be noticed, depending on how much of a dignitary you are. But walk into the same room with a baby in your arms, and the baby will take over as the center of attention. Babies *are* important people. That's because a baby is endowed with all the qualities of personhood, even though many of these must go through a long maturing process.

Have you ever asked what distinguishes us, and our children, as persons? What is there about personhood that is so special?

Personhood is that certain something that distinguishes us as made in "the image of God" (Genesis 1:26,27). We are persons because we are made in the image of the Supreme Person, God, the Creator who made the universe, and who made us! Like God, we can love, have joy, be at peace, exercise patience, and reveal other qualities that are "fruit of the spirit" in our lives. This fruit is the reflection, the confirmation, that God made us in His image. When this fruit is cultivated into Christian graces and true godliness, it is the reflection, the confirmation, that God lives within us. When it is corrupted, it is a confirmation that God does not live within us.

God, of course, has certain qualities or characteristics of His personhood that cannot be reflected in us. They are uniquely part of His personhood. We are not like God in the sense that He is omnipotent (all-powerful), omnipresent (everywhere at once), or omniscient (all-wise). We can create, or be creative, but we are limited to making something from something. God alone can create something from nothing. We can be perfectionists, but I have never met a perfect human. We can be purists, but I have never met a completely pure human. We can strive toward holiness, but God alone is truly holy. We can pass judgment on others, but only God is a righteous judge, discerning good from evil.

God alone has mastery over life and death. Our only claim to victory over death is through His work on the cross through Christ. We can terminate life by murder or suicide, but we cannot originate life. We can participate in procreation, that mysterious process by which God originates human life, but it is God and not we who ultimately brings life into being.

We often permit the dark side of our personhood to prevail. God has no dark side—only light and life and truth. When the Bible speaks of God as angry or jealous it focuses on a righteous God seeking to prevail over unrighteousness. When we are consumed with anger or jealousy we often focus on "our rights" rather than on righteousness.

Our jealousy or anger is too often a spirit of bitterness or a spirit of strife, in search of personal gain rather than a conquest of evil. We allow Satan at times to project his personal qualities upon us. We corrupt the gift of personhood that came from the loving hand of God and allow the dark personhood qualities of the evil one to prevail over the "image of God" within us.

In that wondrous package called personhood, God has endowed us with majestic gifts. One is the gift of worship, or God-consciousness. As far as we know, animals do not have that capacity. They do not worship, they do not seek God through His Word or His Son, they do not pray. That gift distinguishes our personhood from all other creatures, and thus our God-consciousness is a reminder that we are made in the image of God.

In making us persons, God also made us eternal. Our bodies may die, but our persons, who we really are, go on beyond the grave. We will live somewhere, in heaven or hell, after we finish our time on earth. We move from time into eternity. We move from earth to one of those eternal places. Eternal existence distinguishes us from all other creatures. As far as we know, animals do not live beyond this earth.

The fruit of the Spirit (Galatians 5:22,23) also distinguishes us from all other orders of creation. The Spirit of God can bear fruit in our lives, and in that fruitbearing process God reveals His image in us. His fruitfulness is Person-to-person.

Because God is a Person and we are persons, He has created a system by which He and we can communicate the qualities of personhood between us and God and between each other as persons. Through this system we can transmit certain dynamics that build or tear down personhood. God helps us become godly. He helps us as persons become more like Him as a Person, and that in turn enhances our own personhood.

The richest person on earth is one who has permitted God to extend His personhood into his own, and who in return has extended his personhood into God's personhood.

This person-to-person concept which God establishes between His personhood and ours is a grand design which we parents emulate in our relationship with our children. Like God, as we communicate our qualities of personhood to our children, we enhance their personhood. Unlike God, we also enhance our own personhood through this process. We build ourselves as we build others. It is one of the most remarkable concepts on earth. The more we build others through communication, the more we build ourselves.

In most earthly processes, building something depletes the resources necessary to make that object. Build a house and you deplete a supply of lumber, nails, and glass. Build a car and you deplete a supply of steel and plastic. Make a dress and you deplete a supply of cloth and thread. That's the way life is.

But when you build up each other, your peers and your children, you not only don't deplete your own resources but you enhance them. You become a better person, a more effective person, a happier person. Build a child for God and you will likely become a more godly person. It is a breathtaking, unnatural idea. Only God could have thought of it!

To perpetuate God's Person-to-person relationship with us, God established a system of communications. Through His Word, He communicated Himself and what He knows is best for us. Through prayer, He made it possible for us to communicate with Him also. In one sense God's Word is God's personhood verbalized. In that same sense prayer is our attempt to verbalize our personhood to God. In another sense God's Word is His method of extending His personhood into ours. In that same sense prayer is His method by which we extend our personhood into His. Through the reading of His Word and prayer we reveal ourselves Person to-person as well as person-to-Person.

Our communication with God is not so much an exchange between His personhood and our personhood as it is an extension of His personhood into us and an extension of our personhood into Him. Jesus explained this when He said, "If a man remains in me and I in him, he will bear much fruit; apart from me you can do nothing (John 15:5)," and, "Remain in me, and I will remain in you" (John 15:4).

Person-to-person communication through prayer is not merely two people talking to each other. Many people lack power in prayer because they think of prayer as talking to God, and reading the Bible as God talking to them.

When Christ redeems us, He comes and indwells us. God as a Person pitches His tent and dwells within us. But in some remarkable way, at the same time our personhood dwells within Him—His tent in us, ours in Him. As a Person, God extends Himself into us as persons. As a person, we extend ourselves into Him as a Person. That's the message of John 15.

Person-to-person communication concerning parent and child is different. I never indwelt any of my children, nor did they indwell me. In that, God and we are much different.

But because we are made in the image of God, our person-to-person relationship with our children (and our mates) is much more than two distinct and unique personhoods sending messages back and forth, like messengers between two walled cities. I and my children are more than two walled cities with messengers running between us.

Parent/child and husband/wife relationships fall short of indwelling (only God can do that). But they are much more personal than messengers running between walled cities. My wife and I do not indwell each other, nor do we relate like two walled cities. My children and I do not indwell one another, not do we relate like two walled cities. We are distinct, unique persons with the privacy of walled cities. But we are also two persons who reach deeply into each other's lives in love and joy and a building relationship. In that way we emulate God's Person-to-person relationship. We reach into one another deeply, becoming emotionally and spiritually involved, and being so interrelated in mind and spirit that we know what each will say next.

In my person-to-person relationships with my children, I can extend myself into their lives and hopefully they will extend themselves into my life in much the same way. Whenever I am genuinely interested in what my daughter Jan thinks, I ask her. I step into the inner sanctum of her personhood. To be sure, there are doors in there that are marked "private," and I don't knock on them.

Whenever Kathy shows a genuine interest in what I am thinking, she asks me. She steps into the inner sanctum of my personhood. She also does not knock on doors that are marked "private."

Whenever Ron has a personal question or personal idea to share, he feels comfortable in sharing it with me. He steps into my personhood and does not feel he is intruding. Like the others, he would not think of knocking on "private" doors.

Whenever Cindy is hurting or joyful about something, she feels comfortable in sharing her hurts or joys with me (unless it's private). Her hurts become my personal concern because she has brought them not merely to *lay before* me but to *bring into* my personhood.

My children and I are not afraid or ashamed to extend ourselves into one another's personhood, but we are careful not to knock on those doors marked "private." When each of them married, "private" took on new meaning. New facets of their lives went behind "private" doors, and Arlie and I are careful not to knock on them.

Person-to-person communication is the basis, the foundation, for building friendships with your children (and other people as well). Most of us have become accustomed to living life on a nonpersonal plane. We deal with necessities, facts, issues, trivia. But somehow we are afraid to extend our personhood into that of another person—even mates or children.

Think about your conversations this last week, especially your family conversations. How many people have asked you to share your "heartbeat" with them— how you feel, what you are thinking, your hurts and joys, your personal reactions to things close at hand? How many times during this last week have you asked someone concerning their "heartbeat"?

Today when you and your family talk together, take note of what you are saying to one another. Are you exchanging trivia most of the time, or are you truly extending your personhood into theirs, and theirs into yours? Person-to-person communication is trust-building, friendship-building, and life-building.

In summary, here are some guidelines to help us develop a strong person-to-person relationship with our children:

1) We may pattern our parent-child person-to-person relationship after our person-to-Person relationship with God. In doing this, we extend ourselves *into* each other's life, and by doing so we change each other.

2) When we communicate with our children, we must remember that we are not merely two persons talking *to* each other but are two persons involving ourselves *with* each other.

3) Person-to-person conversation does not become preoccupied with externals, but with each other. Through talk, we seek to build one another. Person-to-person communication goes beyond an interest in what the other person *does* and includes what the other person *is*.

5

What Do You Want Your Children to Become?

Remember the well-meaning man who patted you on the head when you were a little boy or girl and asked, "What do you want to be when you grow up?" That's a nervous question, usually asked when an adult doesn't know what else to ask.

You know the standard answers. For a boy it's fireman, policeman, pilot, or big-league athlete. For little boys, these are glamor jobs. Girls might answer with nurse, stewardess, or movie star. Little children have a stereotype concerning these jobs. To a child these are visible people who make things happen. Usually a child thinks of the visibility, such as the uniform, with no conception of the work itself.

Unfortunately, many parents carry similar stereotypes concerning their child's future occupation. Many fathers who dreamed of being a professional ball player push their sons into Little Leagues, often keeping them out of church or Sunday school to do it. There is a hidden purpose here—to live vicariously through the boy. What the father could not do he will try to do through his son.

Have you ever asked yourself what you *really* want your child to be when he or she grows up? Please don't think of a profession or vocation when you ask. That's for your child to decide later on. We parents have no business deciding our child's lifework any more than our parents deciding our own lifework. I think we parents do untold damage if we try to push our children toward any specific job without truly knowing if the child is going to be effective and happy in that job. Let's get out of the business of trying to nudge our children into specific vocations, even vocations that are ministry or missionary oriented. Give God and your child the freedom to work together on those matters.

But as Christian parents there are certain specific goals we should desire for our children as they grow. And we should work with all our energy to see these goals fulfilled in our children. It's part of the God-given responsibility of being a Christian parent.

Let me share some of the goals that Arlie and I have desired for our children (and grandchildren). We have invested our lives to see these goals accomplished, and we believe that is happening. Perhaps you may want these same goals for your children. Or you may have some others.

1) As early as possible, I want my children to come to know God through Christ, to accept Jesus as their own personal Savior.

2) I want them to learn to practice the presence of the living God each day. I want them to grow daily to be more Christlike, more godly.

3) I want them to grow to love God's Word and develop habits of daily Bible reading, not merely because they *should* read it but because they *desire* to read it.

4) I want them to cultivate an effective prayer life, and a life of sharing their faith with others, again, not because they *should* do these things but because they truly *desire* to do them.

5) I want my children to learn to live by biblical values. The Bible presents values such as honesty, faithfulness, truthfulness, generosity, love, patience, obedience, friendliness, self-control, self-confidence, courage, compassion, loyalty, thankfulness, perseverance, and helpfulness. I want them to learn to incorporate these values into their daily decisions and daily conduct. Life at home, in business, in the professions, in government, or wherever or whatever they do should be tempered by these values.

6) I want my children to be men and women of God. I want them to understand what discipleship means, to follow God obediently even when the cost is high.

7) I want them to be exemplary role models as Christians so that other people will desire God because they see God at work winsomely in my children's lives. Their Christian conduct is not to be something stern and demeaning but something beautiful, fragrant, and uplifting. When others watch their conduct they are attracted to Christ, not frightened into His presence.

8) I want my children to be effective in their chosen work. I do not want to choose that work for any one of them, or even lead them against their will, or subtly campaign for them to enter into a work in which they will be less than happy or less than effective. But I do hope they will do their best at whatever work they choose. And I do trust they will stay away from vocations that would not bring honor to God.

9) I want my children to put their mates and their children at the highest order of priority in their lives. I've learned that family is basic, and that happiness

depends on getting family in the rightful place of priority ahead of other things. I hope my children put no one but God above their family.

10) I want my children to adopt God's priorities for service. If they choose to live in modest circumstances to serve God in a certain way, that is a noble choice, and I would applaud them for it. If they choose to serve God under uncomfortable circumstances, I will pray with them for God's grace to endure. If they choose service that is not a "Christian vocation," but still have a heart to serve God, I will consider them God's servants.

11) I want my children to be good stewards of their resources. If they receive a modest income, I hope they will manage their modesty well. If the windows of heaven open and pour out abundance upon them, I hope they will remain modest and generous as they manage their abundance. I want them to be good stewards of whatever God gives them. I have seen wealth corrupt devout Christians and make them proud and arrogant. If I knew this would happen to any of my children, I would beg God to withhold wealth from them. My prayer is that God will give my children all that they can prayerfully use for His honor, but never a measure of abundance that will corrupt them. God alone knows where that boundary is.

Forty years ago I asked God to let me serve Him in a career ministry. From what I had seen, I expected to live in near-poverty. Arlie married me with that understanding, so she also expected that we would live in near-poverty (that's a wonderful test of love!). For some reason God has given us far more than we ever expected, and I'm grateful for this. I believe I could have been thoroughly happy if I had lived in near-poverty, as long as I was doing what God wanted me to do. Now that I have more than I expected, I feel that I have a greater burden to be a good steward. What I have is not mine to keep but God's resources put in my trust to manage. I really want to be a good steward. I want my children to be good stewards.

12) I pray that my children will keep money in proper perspective. I pray that they will keep earning and spending and giving in proper perspective. I pray that they will never be consumed with earning so much that they will neglect God or their family. I want them to keep the pursuit of resources and the careful management of resources in balance. I want them to keep resources and family in balance. I pray that they will never be consumed with the desire to be wealthy for the sake of wealth, but that if it should come, they will be consumed with the desire to gratefully manage their wealth for God in a way that will please Him.

13) I want my children to be disciplined people. I want them to understand that, like monetary resources, their lives are a trust from God, to be managed carefully for the greatest good and the greatest effectiveness.

14) I want my children to enter into the delights of life with enthusiasm. I want them to appreciate their God-given senses, to enjoy the beauties of His handiwork, to be grateful for the scene of the rose or the taste of pancakes on a winter morning. I want them to delight in taking their children out in the forest to appreciate the leaves and wildflowers, the birds and woodland creatures, to gaze in awe at the clouds in the sky, to be delighted with the sunset and the harvest moon rising in the autumn sky. I want my children to enthusiastically impart these values to their children and thereby impart an affinity with the Creator through the enjoyment of His footprints and fingerprints.

15) I want my children to look at life with a proper mixture of seriousness and good humor. There is a time to walk into God's presence with a hush. There is a time to laugh uproariously—yes, even laugh at ourselves and our strange ways. I believe that God has a sense of humor, and I hope my children will also maintain a sense of humor. There have been many times when my children and I have laughed about some ridiculous thing we have said or done.

16) I want my children to be redemptive with their lives. That is, I want them to be *life-changers*. When they do something I hope they will do it for God, or for another person, but not for self primarily. Self-preservation at all costs is self-destruction. Our very growth as Christians requires that we invest our lives redemptively for God and others.

17) In their work, I want my children to be servant leaders. As Christ came to serve, so they and I as Christians are called to be Christlike, and that requires us to serve as He served.

Having listed all of these wonderful things that I want my children (and grandchildren) to become, how do I help them reach these objectives, assuming that they too want to reach them?

I could outline these objectives for my children and tell them that this is what I want, and perhaps make a manual and go over it daily, or hang this list over the doorway of their room. I could tell them that this is what I want them to become and they had better shape up and do it. I could nag them daily to fulfill my expectations. But you who are parents know that this is entirely the opposite way to accomplish goals such as these.

How can we ask children to become kind and loving and patient, for example, if we try to force them to be kind and loving and patient? No, that would not work. I have seen parents try this approach, and it backfires, turning child against parent. You cannot force anyone to love something! You cannot force anyone to desire something (unless he desires that you would get off his back).

There is another way. I could outline these objectives for my children and plead with them to accomplish them. I could beg them daily for my sake and theirs, and even for God's sake, to do these things. Perhaps I could even shed a few tears. I could lay a guilt trip on them. But you parents also know that this will not work. You simply cannot lead children to be kind, loving, and patient by making them feel guilty or making them feel that they are doing it to please you. No, that will not work much better than trying to force them to be kind, loving, and patient.

But there is a way. As parents, we may role-model our goals for them, living out these goals in our own lives. If these goals are important for your children, they are equally important for you. You will stress their importance by making them your own goals. Your children will want to be like you when you model these goals, because they will see that you truly believe in these goals and are trying to make them happen in your own life. Our lives as role models become testimonials rather than commandments. "Don't do as I do, do as I say" will send your children down the road in the opposite direction.

When we live out our goals for our children in our own lives, we gravitate naturally to daily conversation that focuses on these things. We can talk with our children with ease about what it means to live out these goals in daily living because we are already experiencing these things in our lives and our children are observing us. If they see that we are living what we are saying, they will listen. If they see that we are not living what we are saying, they will think we are mocking them. Perhaps we are!

Our conversations about these goals are not contrived, formal, stiff-talk times. We look for opportunities to talk about God in the context of the delights of living. On a radio interview one day a thoughtless mother said to me that she had two-hour devotionals with her children each day. I asked how they kept quiet that long. She said she had a big wooden spoon and when they lost attention she would whack them with it.

That poor deluded mother will wonder someday why her children turn against Christianity and her. They never knew the delights of a daily walk with the Lord—only the stern disciplines. We must all experience the delights of walking in His presence daily; then the disciplines actually become delights.

Do you remember the Golden Rule? "In everything, do to others what you would have them do to you" (Matthew 7:12). Sometimes we phrase it "Do unto others as you would have them do unto you."

The Golden Rule says, "Decide what you want others to do to you, then first do that to them." It does not say, "Do unto others *so that* they will do unto you." Nor does it say, "Do unto others *as they do* unto you."

The message is clear: Our conduct to others is what we want others' conduct to be toward us. The Golden Rule is most golden in our own homes with our own families.

In summary, here are three simple guidelines for Christian parents in helping children become what you want them to be (and what you think God wants them to be):

1) As early as possible in your child's life, decide what you want your child to become, not vocationally but personally, and commit these goals into writing.

2) Make these your own personal goals so that your child will see you live them out each day as a role model.

3) Develop conversations in the context of the delights of daily living, focusing on these goals. Each day learn to talk about these things rather than trivia only. Of course you will also talk about trivia, for life is filled with trivia, often necessary trivia. But as you live out the goals for your children, and see them lived out in your children's lives, you *will* want to talk about them.

6

Talk Is Mutual Acceptance

A dozen years ago Arlie and I were in rural Turkey, about a stone's throw from the Syrian border. This was one of several photo missions we took in the Middle East, photographing Bible sites and lifestyles reminiscent of Bible life and times.

Miles from nowhere we came across an encampment that reminded us of Abraham's early home. Camels, donkeys, tents, sheep—they were all there. It was a photographer's dream. I jumped from our little car and began to take pictures. But my dreams were soon shattered when a man much larger than I appeared with a giant staff in his hands. He was angry and began to shout at me in what I assume was either Arabic or Turkish.

This wild-looking man was talking *to* me, I know that. But he never talked *with* me.

It was clear that he was not accepting me. And it was equally clear that he did not want me to accept him. He wanted me to get out of there as fast as I could. Needless to say, that's exactly what I did!

On another occasion on the West Bank, we were looking for the little village of Anata and stopped to ask a Bedouin, dressed in full costume, sitting on a stone fence. I pointed to three neighboring villages and asked in a broken, condescending English "Anata?" as I pointed to each in turn. The man smiled and spoke in better English than I, "That village over there is Anata!" I felt stupid.

Then the man invited us to his tent, some 12 miles away toward the Jordan River. Unlike other Bedouin we have visited, he introduced us to his wife and shared cups of sour goats' milk with us. This man talked *with* us. He accepted us with his hospitality. We also talked *with* him, and accepted his hospitality. There was mutual acceptance. This meeting was quite different from our encounter near the Turkish-Syrian border.

These two encounters are similar to our own encounters with one another. Sometimes we accept one another and carry on conversations that reveal and enhance that acceptance. At other times we reject one another and our conversations reveal that rejection. Even as parents we gravitate back and forth between acceptance and rejection of our children.

Mary comes home with a good report card and we shift into an acceptance mode. Tom spills ink on the living-room carpet and we move into a rejection mode. Bill volunteers to mow the lawn for us and we move back into the acceptance mode. Janet breaks an antique dish and we flop back into a rejection mode.

Sometimes our rejection is mini-rejection and sometimes it is maxi-rejection. Sometimes we move toward mini-acceptance and sometimes toward maxi-acceptance. Sometimes our acceptance or rejection is short-term, while at other times we carry on for days, weeks, or even months.

Rejection may manifest itself in a wide assortment of responses. I'm told that child abuse is one form of rejection (an extreme form, to be sure). Silence is another form—a rather harsh form, you'll agree, if you've ever been given the silent treatment. If I were a child I think I could endure abuse almost as much as silence or shunning. Both of these strip the child of a sense of personal worth and even of personhood itself.

Building a child—that is, helping a child grow to maturity as a young man or woman of God—is a process of mutual acceptance. The parent-child relationship of mutual acceptance is a reflection of the parent-God relationship of mutual acceptance. Growing in God is recognizing that God fully accepts us. But it also is fully accepting Him. The cross is the focal point of God accepting us. The altar is the symbolic focal point of our accepting God through Christ.

I mentioned earlier a man who was rejected by his father when he was a boy. His father daily made it clear to him that he was not fully a son—that he was someone to be ridiculed and hammered and mocked. It was not surprising that when this boy grew to be a man he rejected his father. Rejection is the seed that grows into the tree of rejection, which in turn produces the seed of rejection, which grows into the tree of rejection.

Jesus said, "If anyone is ashamed of me and my words in this adulterous and sinful generation, the Son of Man will be ashamed of him when he comes in his Father's glory with the holy angels" (Mark 8:38). Jesus was saying that He must reject anyone who rejects Him. Being accepted of God is a two-way street—we accept Him and He accepts us.

We parents reveal our acceptance or rejection of our children by the way we talk with them. At one extreme, silence or shunning is total rejection. It says, "I will not verbally acknowledge that you are a person. I will not talk with you at all." If you or I believed that God totally rejected us in His silence, we would have no hope for the future. When a child believes that a parent is totally rejecting him in silence, a spirit of hopelessness prevails.

But at the other end of the spectrum, there is mutual acceptance through conversation (talk) between parent and child. When our children sit down with us to talk, the coffeepot bubbles and we laugh together about little things (and sometimes cry together about other things), but we walk into one another's personhood and explore the depths of what each other is thinking.

At that moment the other person is king or queen. We celebrate each other's presence and personhood. We acknowledge that for this wonderful time of mutual exploration there is no more important person in all the world than the person across the table from us. All work ceases, all of life's urgencies are held in suspense, all chores come to a grinding halt, all "shoulds" and "hope-tos" and "could-dos" that keep us busy are put aside.

Knowing that you are supremely important to another person is a building time; knowing that all work and activity will be set aside to celebrate your presence is constructive. That is acceptance of the highest order. When two people *mutually* celebrate each other's personhood, something truly special happens.

I believe that the lack of this mutual celebration of personhood is a root cause of divorce. It may well be a root cause of teen rebellion, runaways, and drug use. When we come to believe that work or things or money or anything else is more important than us, we lose that sense of acceptance and our roots, and with that loss we lose a proper self-evaluation.

Mutual acceptance, mutual celebration of personhood, builds a wholesome sense of self because it tells the person across the table from you that he or she is more important that anything in the world at that moment. Nothing will compete for your attention while you and that person are talking.

Of course, you must truly believe this. You must cultivate the power of personhood and the priority of personhood. It is not something that happens suddenly tomorrow afternoon.

That's why it is so vital for parents to develop this gift of mutual acceptance through mutual talk as children grow up. Day by day, brick by brick, you will build in them a self-confidence and a strong parent-child relationship that will last a lifetime. This is one of the truly lasting gifts you can give your child. It is a heritage bestowed, richer than the gift of royalty.

In summary, here are some guidelines in establishing mutual acceptance through talking with your child:

1) Helping a child grow to be a strong man or woman of God is a process of mutual acceptance through talking together as parent and child.

2) How we talk with our child reveals how we accept our child. When you talk with your child, make him or her the most important person in your life at that moment.

3) The best way to prevent ruptured relationships that terminate in runaways, rebellion, drugs, or undesirable friends is to cultivate daily talk with your child that reaches your personhood into your child's personhood and helps the child to know that talking with him or her is your highest priority during that time.

7

A Child Is a Child,
But More than a Child

Do you remember ET? Not too many years ago we saw this lovable little fellow from another planet visit our movie screens and befriend an ordinary suburban boy. ET and his friend could not talk with each other with words, but they communicated warmth and friendship. The movie became very popular and its creator earned millions of dollars from it.

I've asked myself at least a dozen times what made this movie so popular. Why did these two childlike creatures win the hearts (and loosen the purse strings) of so many people? On the one hand it was a majestic theme—interplanetary communication, a story of two worlds that met face-to-face, a hint of intragalactic diplomacy. On the other hand it was a simple theme—two little kids playing in the backyard. The story was the confluence of these two streams, the majestic and the ordinary.

Did you learn what I think I learned from this? I think this movie would have been a dud if it had been the same story except with a full-grown suburbanite man and a full-grown extraterrestrial being.

I think also that it would not have worked if the movie had tried to solve majestic themes with majestic means, or ordinary themes with ordinary means. Childlikeness was the understatement of enormous power behind the scenes. What nations and worlds and galaxies could not accomplish in military power and grand diplomatic schemes, two little "kids" in the backyard could.

Did we like this movie because of this portrait of the power of childlikeness, because of the grandeur of simplicity, because of interplanetary statesmanship reduced to its essence—simple, personal love and trust? I think so. ET and his earthling friend developed a bond of love and trust, even without words, because they interacted without complication.

We adults drown in words, but we can't communicate because we try to complicate simplicity. As adults we unlearn what we knew so well as a child.

I have moved among intellectuals and I have moved among children. I have profound regard for my intellectual friends. We need them. Shame on any segment of the church that ridicules them (and I have known that to happen). They delve into depths that most of us cannot comprehend and converse at heights we cannot imagine. No, we need our intellectuals, for they are in the business of idea formation, and that is the basis for a full, rich society. I trust that all of us who do not claim to be intellectuals will be gracious and loving toward this important segment of society.

But I trust that my intellectual friends will be equally accepting and gracious toward those of us who spend our days among our children. I have heard demeaning comments such as "Sunday school stuff" or "kid stuff," which was a way of saying it was trite. People snort at something as "Mickey Mouse," another way of saying trite. The implication is that anything at a child's level is trite, while anything at the intellectual level is profound.

I've never said this in a book before—in fact I have never said this publicly before—but I must say it to give context. I have earned three master's degrees and two doctor's degrees, one from a seminary and one from a major university, so I have drunk from the wells of the intellectuals. That does not make me an intellectual, of course. I don't claim to be.

Most of my lifetime has been spent developing books and curriculum for children. I say these two things to emphasize that I have lived in both worlds. I must say this to point out that I am not analyzing or criticizing worlds in which I have not lived.

Some of you reading this book are career housewives and mothers. I have heard you speak of yourselves as "just a housewife" or "just a mother." There are no "justa" people in God's creation. Each of us has our unique task to do. If being a housewife is your chosen career, you can do it with excellence as much as a president of a large corporation can do his or her work with excellence.

If being a mother is your chosen career, you can leave a product (your child) to influence the world as much as the most astute intellectual or the most visible politician. Your product may not be as visible as another, but it may be much more lasting.

In my family we can trace Christian influence at least eight generations back from my grandchildren, who are heirs of that influence. In Arlie's family we know of at least five consecutive generations of strong Christian influence through parents and their children. To us, family is the strongest and most effective Christian institution we know. The influence of godly mothers and fathers in those families has made profound, lasting footprints.

If every Christian couple would leave behind three godly children who never witnessed beyond their family (and a faithful witness will reach beyond family, of course), the witness of Christ would grow 50 percent (compounded) with every generation, which quite obviously is not happening. If this were true, we would have won the world to Christ generations ago. We wouldn't need as many Christian institutions to pick up the pieces. We would not need as much government, as many social institutions, or as many prisons. Society would be leavened in a remarkable way. I may be wrong, but I think we Christians are spending too much time on less important things than our children, thinking they are more important because they are "bigger."

I call for Christian parents to be Christian parents— to see clearly the significance of Christian parenting, and to give our full attention and devotion to this task as much as we would to becoming effective businessmen or professionals.

I call you to see your children in context with the Great Commission as a higher calling than any other. I call you to see your children and their potential witness through their children and beyond through the generations. I call you to see your involvement with your children as infinitely more important than the TV programs you will watch this week, the golf game you will play this week, the lunch you may have with a business partner this week, and the time you may spend with your friends this week.

I'm not asking you to give up these things if you are spending the time and energies you should with your children. But are you spending the time and energies you should with your children?

When you are dealing with your children you are not dealing with insignificance; instead, you are the narrow neck of the funnel through which the future of the world is being poured. The entire world of the next generation (and generations beyond) depends on what you and your parental peers do with your children in this generation.

That's not "kid stuff"—it's world power! And that world power will come to focus tonight when your little child crawls up on your lap and says, "Tell me a story" or, "Read to me." Or when your child wants to cuddle or wants comfort when someone has teased him.

So how do we perpetuate this Christian influence through our children? I believe it is primarily through our talk with them. It's what we say and how we say it, and it's how we back up our verbal talk with our "conduct talk," our role-modeling.

If you think of your children as small and unimportant, you will talk with them about small, insignificant matters. You will communicate trivia to them. And their growth will reflect this dimension of talk. You will leave behind a generation of stunted dwarfs.

On the other hand, if you see your children as future parents, future leaders, future men and women of God, and see them as growing daily toward this important role, you will do all in your power to shape their lives toward the grand objective of helping them become parents, leaders, and men and women of God. Your conversation will point toward that end.

I know this sounds lofty and idealistic, but it's time we parents began to think of the ideals of parenting. Really, it works! I know it does, because I have seen it work. But it does cost time and energy. It costs a commitment to the task. It forces us to put our priorities in order and be willing to put aside things we merely think are important for things we know are important.

We must not see our work with children as building for the future alone. I believe childhood is one of our most important periods of all life. We must delight in childhood for the sake of childhood. As we choose our reading material and our talks with our children, we are in part training them for the future and we are in part helping them delight in each stage of childhood as they go through it.

We have a tendency to rush childhood (some call it the loss of childhood or vanishing childhood). We sometimes try to force our children to grow up too fast. Let's not do that. Let's help our first-grade child delight in those things which delight a first-grader. Let's help our fourth-grade child delight in those things which delight a fourth-grader.

So we are keeping one eye to the future and making sure that we are preparing our child to become the man or woman of God that we want them to be (and God wants them to be). But we are keeping the other eye on the present to help our child delight in the things of childhood now.

I like child-dedication services in our churches because they speak of parental commitment to the task of raising the child for God. They speak also of the role of Christians in the body of Christ to support one another in this important task. In our church we as a congregation pledge to help the parents who are dedicating their children. Our pledge is that we are there to help, we are there to back them up in the role of parenting.

Back to the story of the movie ET. As I said, I think the success of this story was recognizing that big themes and important matters are wrapped up in the essence of childhood. The author of this script recognized an important truth that is a biblical truth, but often ignored by Christian parents. Jesus said it: "Of such is the kingdom of God" (Mark 10:14 KJV).

In summary, here are some guidelines to help us see the enormous potential and power invested in little children:

1) Because a child is little does not mean that he is unimportant. God has invested enormous power for the future in each little child. Shaping a child's life for God is an act of power, influencing the world for Christ for generations to come.

2) As parents we need to get our priorities straight, recognizing that the time we spend with our children is perhaps the richest investment of time and energy that we can make. That investment is much more important than many others we think are "big" investments.

3) Parenting is a commitment of ourselves to the task of guiding our children. We can't delegate the task to others. Only *we* can do it, and it requires our devotion and energy and delight in order to do it well. But the rewards are eternal.

4) We guide our children in God's ways by talking about God's ways. It is through our talk with our children that we help to shape their lives for God.

8

Quality One-on-One Time

Arlie and I have five children, and our parenting spans 35 years. As you can imagine, in a house filled with five children growing up, life was like a zoo—a happy zoo, but a zoo nevertheless. From morning to night there was a high energy level.

Our children were involved in music, athletics, church activities, and school activities. This meant that *we* were involved in music, athletics, church activities, and school activities. We tried to be there at every event for every child. When you multiply all those things by five, that's a lot of going to events!

It's easy in a busy household like ours to become consumed with the dynamic of the group. It's difficult to find the time, or should I say *take* the time, to develop quality one-on-one relationships with each of the five children. But those are the times that were truly special.

I believe that families should cultivate activities of togetherness. Travel together, take picnics and hikes together, go as a family to a son's little league game, go as a family to a daughter's recital. Participating in each other's activities welds a family together.

But there must also be a time for parent and child to have some quality one-on-one time. Looking back, I wish we would have done more of this. I know we did much more than many of our friends have done, but I think we should have done even more than we did.

Let me share some wonderful times I remember. These are but a few of the hundreds that I could share. One day Kathy and I sprawled in the grass in our backyard and talked about the Indians who once lived there on our place. We knew that was true because we have found Indian relics in our little woods. We talked of the braves who went out to hunt, some returning with deer (which still roam the hills near our home), some returning empty-handed. We talked of the squaw who was sick and of the old Indian who died one winter in the tepee on the hill where we sat. We talked of babies born and babies that grew sick, of how they ate and how they played. It was mostly pure imagination, but each of us fed the other's imagination.

When Jan was little, I loved to go into our backyard woods with her at times and help her pick violets and anemones. When we traveled, and it was Arlie's time to drive, we often crawled into the back of the station wagon and challenged each other with a game of names and associations. She might say, "Hi, Sandy," and I would answer, "Where's the beach?" Or I would say, "Hi, Bill," and she would answer, "Why don't you pay?" I know it's corny, but we had an incredible amount of fun.

I remember days when Cindy and I walked through the vacant field across from our home, looking for Indian relics. Finding a relic spurs conversation about the Indians and who left that relic behind, what were the last hands to touch it, and what that person was doing. When did that Indian lose the relic? Was it winter or summer? Was he hunting and carelessly dropped it, or did a squaw drop it in some weeds and couldn't find it?

During her college years Cindy has come home every weekend (she's 20 miles away). We always get out the coffeepot, and Arlie and I both talk with her, or else just one of us talks with her. We'll often talk for an hour at a time.

The big thing with Ron or Doug was for me to go into our yard and toss the football to them, or bat a softball for them to catch. Through the years, from the time they were each little boys, we spent hundreds of hours doing that. We built a treehouse. We looked for acorns in the woods. We played games. I always wanted to set up a workshop and build a canoe with them, but that's something we left as a dream only.

Ron and Doug were involved in Little League softball, so Arlie and I got involved in it. We went to every game, and as we chauffeured each of them to and from games and practice, we had many hours of one-on-one time (and sometimes two-on-two time) to talk about those things.

Doug became interested in political campaign buttons, and we helped him collect them, frame them, and hang them in his room. There were play times with model trains, Indian relic hunts, and canoe rides, as well as times to wrestle on the floor.

It's a spectator sport, I know, but through the years my sons and I often watched pro ball (baseball or football) together. It was a threesome rather than one-on-one, but we had enormous fun chatting about the games, the plays made, and what we would have done to improve on a certain play (spectators can always improve on a pro athlete!).

Doug has graduated into the presence of our Lord, taken at age 26 in an auto accident. We miss his robust laughter and clever comments as Ron and Brad (Kathy's husband) and I now watch the Chicago Cubs or Chicago Bears play through their seasons. We try to get together almost once each week to do this. We can't watch a game in silence; that's not the way it's done. We cheer and shout and have as many comments back and forth as the announcer.

Now that Ron is an editor in a publishing company, it's not surprising that he and I can talk by the hour about ideas for publishing. Talking is not something new; we've done it since he was born.

It's not surprising that each month Arlie and I talk on the phone for hours with our children. We meet here at our house each Sunday we can for Sunday dinner and spend the rest of the day together talking, playing games, or having fun. Our grandchildren have joined us now, so a new circle of talk has begun.

For us, a fire in the fireplace on a winter day is an invitation to sit and talk. Or a walk in the woods is a great time to ponder things together. Chauffeuring children to and from music lessons, recitals, games, and school events can be a time to grumble or drive in silence, or else it can be a grand opportunity to talk heart-to-heart, mind-to-mind, life-to-life with a child.

Mealtime is a grand time to talk together, not about the complaints of the day or the disciplines of the family, but about things that build us up as persons, things that all family members can enjoy. When children are small, mealtime is not the time for mother and father to talk about finances or business, which children hear with utter boredom.

If you look for them, there are many "lost" hours which could be turned into wonderful one-on-one times of conversation, especially those hours in the car, or at home, when we might grumble that we are "stuck with our kids." Redeem those moments and hours with talk!

When Arlie was growing up, she and her sisters used dishwashing time as a special time to not only talk together but sing together. Out of this "dishpan rehearsal" came a quartet (later a trio) which sang at many church services and civic events and then became the college girls' trio. It also produced a life-long close friendship among the sisters, *and* their children.

When I grew up on a farm in the postdepression years we could not afford to go anywhere or do anything in the evening after the chores were done. So we all sat on the front porch and talked the evening away. Looking back, our near-poverty was a marvelous glue that helped bind our family together.

My friend (and one of our pastors) Mike Nelson has a great one-on-one tradition with his three sons. Periodically he takes one son alone to breakfast in a restaurant to talk. Mike is a busy man, much in demand as a speaker. It would be easy for him to neglect his family. But he has put his priorities straight, with family first—an example to other ministers and any other family.

Why is one-on-one time so important? Put two people in a room and you will hear one type of conversation. Add a third person and the conversation will take an abrupt 90-degree turn. One-on-one is intimacy, heart-to-heart, mind-to-mind, person-to-person. Marriages are failing today because husbands and wives have lost the art of one-on-one talk, the intimacy of talk. Parents and children are drifting because they do not cultivate this one-on-one relationship of person-to-person closeness.

A domestic-relations lawyer was asked, "What is the single biggest reason couples split up?" His answer: "Their inability to talk with each other, bare their souls, and treat each other as best friend." This man had spent 28 years practicing divorce law, so he should know. He went on to say that couples talk mostly about superficial things to impress each other. This brings on infidelity, drinking, and physical or mental abuse.

Since this is true with couples (and if we think of couples whose marriages are in trouble we *know* it is true), it is equally true with parent-child relationships. We could rephrase the question someone asked the domestic relations lawyer, "What is the single biggest reason that parents and children develop tensions?" I think the answer would remain the same: Their inability to talk with each other, bare their souls, and treat each other as best friend.

Talk is the vehicle by which we develop that rich person-to-person relationship necessary to keep husbands and wives or parents and children on the same track. And quality one-on-one time to talk is essential to develop that heart-to-heart and mind-to-mind relationship called intimacy.

Quality one-on-one time helps a child discover himself or herself. As a society we are consumed with groupthink, the mindset of the crowd. Television rarely enriches our individuality because it cannot deal with our individuality. TV producers are consumed with what certain segments of society think, what the trends among groups of people are, and how they can motivate or captivate the mind of the masses. TV producers can't even consider what you as an individual think. Their success is built on ratings, and ratings are trends among groups of people. An individual in this process is a monolithic image of a collection of individuals who represent one mindset.

Politics builds itself on groupthink. Do you recall what happened on the night of the last national political election? There was debate about the ethics of TV news departments declaring winners before the West

Coast polls had closed. How could they do this? They didn't know how millions of people had voted yet. The answer is that they have developed the art of sampling the mindset of a few and projecting it across the nation. They understand groupthink in the political process and are able to project how a small sample of thinking early in the evening represents the entire nation. Actually, through these samplings, they know the mindset of the voting public before they even vote.

Athletics builds on groupthink. A batter knocks the ball over the fence for a home run. What happens? The entire crowd of fans for that team screams and shouts and waves their arms as one person. Thousands of people are of one mindset, without shame or criticism. A football player recovers a fumble, or intercepts a pass, or makes a touchdown. The reaction is predictable. You've seen it dozens of times.

I'm sorry to say that much of our educational system plays to the groupthink concept. I personally do not like the SAT and ACT testing systems because I have seen brilliant young men or women who did not fit the mold but had enormous talents that could not be tested this way. These tests have their purpose, but they also have enormous limitations. Intelligence tests do not test overall intelligence but only certain facets of intelligence. From what I have read of Einstein, I think he might not have been accepted at many of our colleges because he might not have done well on these tests.

I don't have an adequate solution for this problem, because admissions directors at our colleges must have some type of objective criteria for admitting students. But in my opinion (and it is an opinion shared by many people I have talked with), we are losing some brilliant students who do not fit the mold because they don't think a certain way that people are "supposed" to think.

In my opinion this is also a serious flaw in American education. We spend too little time helping individuals discover themselves and develop themselves as individuals, and too much time pressuring them to conform to the group. Again, I don't have a good solution because our teachers are overworked now and cannot possibly give the attention necessary to each individual. So we continue to train the individual to conform to the group rather than enhance individuality.

Even in the workplace we must conform to the company image and company policy and company program. We have few places in the job market for true individualists.

The church is not free from this same problem. Too many churches demand conformity and build systems of guilt if we do not conform in every way. Of course we must agree on the fundamentals of the faith, for that is the basis for the existence of the church. But we have forced conformity on little things that are not at all related to the fundamentals of the faith.

As parents we face the frustration of helping our children learn to fit the mold (and fit the mold they must if they are to succeed) and yet to learn to be individuals, to think for themselves.

Leadership requires individuality. No one ever rose to a position of highest leadership without the ability to be an individual, to think for himself or herself. But where does a person learn this? I think mostly in the home, with parents who help the child to think independently rather than in groupthink terms.

Of all mind-building, life-building, soul-stretching relationships on earth, I believe there is no more effective one than a quality one-on-one relationship with a Christian parent. These are times when the growing child learns who he is, who the parent is, and who God is. For a child to learn how to be most effective as a Christian, he must learn these three.

Also, one-on-one is the basis for a growing child's security. A parent who is *for* you is the rock-solid foundation on which a secure self-image is built. If a child knows that he can always count on a parent to be there, to be *for* him, he can know that even though the whole world is against him, he will always have a secure refuge from life's storms. Secure refuges provide secure self-image. We must know that there is a place to retreat when life turns against us.

As we grow we learn more and more that God is our refuge (Deuteronomy 33:27). He is a shelter in the storms of life. He is the One with ever-present, always-open arms to receive us. He is always there, always listening, always *for* us. To the child, this image of God is projected through the parent. The child learns about God by interacting with a godly parent each day.

Quality one-on-one interaction is not a recent development; it is the biblical expression of God's relationship available for us. Stop now and read Psalm 23, and as you do, think about the Lord's quality one-on-one relationship with you, and how each verse expresses that relationship.

Now ponder how Psalm 23 is a prototype of your own quality one-on-one relationship with your child. May I paraphrase Psalm 23 as a Psalm for a Parent, God's undershepherd, this way:

A PSALM FOR A PARENT
Adapted from Psalm 23

I am God's shepherd for my child,
   put here to supply all his needs.
I help my child lie down
      where he will be safe and secure,
      and I lead him to quiet, untroubled places
         where his soul will be restored.
I guide my child in paths of righteousness
      for God's sake and his own.
Even when my child walks through
      dark and difficult places,
         he does not need to be afraid,
            because I am with him, and that comforts him.
I provide all the good food my child needs,
      even when his "friends" who want
         to hurt him are nearby.
I treat him like a young prince or princess,
      and bring a rich family heritage to him.
As long as my child lives,
      I will always be his friend,
         sharing kindness and good things.
I will be a leader and role model for my child,
      so that at the end of life we will
         live together in God's heavenly home.

In summary, here are some guidelines to help you provide quality one-on-one conversation with your child:

1) As families we need to do many things together, but we also need times of quality one-on-one conversation to build one another.

2) We may find many lost moments, even hours, where we can have that quality one-on-one conversation—hours when we ride together in the car, eat together at the table, or do chores together, hours otherwise given to trivia.

3) Quality one-on-one conversation builds intimacy, and intimacy is essential in building lasting friendships between husband and wife or parent and child.

4) Quality one-on-one conversation helps a child discover who he is, who his parent is, and who God is, and these are all essentials of godly living.

5) Quality one-on-one conversation frees a child from the restraints of groupthink, so prevalent in our society, and helps him build individuality, essential to leadership.

6) Quality one-on-one conversation provides a child with needed security, which promotes a healthy self-image. It is this self-image which helps the child face the storms of life unafraid, for the lingering presence of parent and the Lord are with him.

9

Are Your Attitudes Beatitudes?

Jane and Joan live next door to each other. Each has three children. Both are going with their children on a school field trip to the zoo.

"I'll be glad when this day is over," said Jane. "It's no fun ushering a bunch of screaming kids around a smelly zoo."

"Oh, we don't feel that way about it," said Joan. "My children and I are excited about this trip. We have been reading together about the different animals we will see. And each day we talk about the fun we'll have together."

Jane and Joan will do the same activity today. But it will be a much different day for them. It will also be a much different day for their children.

Jane sees the trip as a chore, a responsibility she has to do, and will be glad when her chore is done. Joan sees the trip as an opportunity for fun and learning. She will be glad to participate in the trip. Both she and her children will learn much and delight much in the day. They will remember the zoo, and the day, with fondness. Jane's children will remember it, but with not so much fondness.

What's the difference? Attitude. Jane and Joan are about the same age, same economic circumstances, same neighborhood, same school, similar children, really not much difference in lifestyle. But their attitudes are poles apart.

Would it surprise you to look ahead through the years and see their children's attitudes poles apart?

A story I heard many years ago sums up the word "attitude." I have heard this story with many variations, but this is the one I like best.

One day a man approached a building site where three stonemasons were working. "What are you doing?" he asked the first. The stonemason's brow was furrowed and he looked burdened. "I'm working hard to earn a living," he grumbled. "That's all I do— work, work, work! I can't wait to get out of here and get home at night."

"What are you doing?" he asked the second stonemason. "I'm laying up stones," he said. "It's a good job, pays well, has good benefits, and I'll be able to retire on schedule."

"What are you doing?" the man asked the third stonemason. The man looked up with a smile. His face glowed. "I'm building a cathedral," he said.

Three men, all doing the same work, with the same pay. Everything was the same—everything except attitude.

"I can't wait to get this job done," one person in your company says.

"I can't wait to do this job," says another.

Both get the same salary, same benefits, same boss, same work. Things are all the same—except attitude. The second person will advance with higher pay and greater job satisfaction. The first will find a new job where he can continue to grumble. The difference? Attitude.

What is attitude? It is a rather elusive part of our personhood. I've thought of a dozen definitions, but I'm not sure that any of them quite captures the essence of attitude. Let me try a few, though, to see if we can get at the idea.

1) Attitude is outlook reflected in the mirror of inlook. How we look at ourselves determines how we look at all we encounter in life.

2) Attitude is our personal disk operating system (for the benefit of you computer buffs). All personal programs operate from that base.

3) Attitude is the magic window through which we view life. When the window is clouded we see a clouded world. When it is bright and sparkling, we see a world that is bright and sparkling.

4) Attitude is the scale on which we weigh life's values, helping us gauge the importance of what we think, say, and do.

5) Attitude is the filter through which we pour self-image into the cup of experience. How we experience what we experience is determined by the condition of the filter.

6) Attitude is the clothing worn by personhood. The world around us sees either a bum or a beauty, not so much because they assess our inner condition but because they perceive our outer expression.

As a father and grandfather I have pondered my legacy to the next two generations. What do I want to leave most with my sons, daughters, grandsons, and granddaughters? Among many good gifts, I would like to bestow on these generations the right attitude toward life.

My mirror is a rather brash, insolent piece of furniture. It mocks me. When I get up in the morning and look in the mirror it responds exactly the way I project myself to it. When I frown, it frowns. When I smile, it smiles. When I look gloomy, it looks gloomy. When I project sunshine, it projects sunshine.

People I meet are like my mirror. When I am cranky, so are people who respond to me. When I smile and project a ray of sunshine, it bounces right back from people around me.

One day I noticed that some total strangers were smiling at me. I wondered if I had forgotten to comb my hair or wash my face. But when I checked, everything was in order. What was it? As I reflected back, I think I must have smiled at them first. They were merely responding. Have you ever had this experience?

Our faces reflect the attitudes that people around us project. Their faces reflect the attitudes we project. We condition one another by our attitudes. We can either be clouds or sunshine for those around us.

Think how much more we parents condition the attitudes of our children who spend most of their time with us and depend on us to shape their early lives! Our children's formative years include the formation of attitude. Much of their later adult attitude may come from your present adult attitude.

Here's a mini-experiment. The next time you see one of your children, smile but don't say a word, then see what happens. Your child will likely smile back. If you frown, even in silence, your child will likely frown back. Now think how many hundreds of times you smile or frown through your child's countenance each year.

But smiles and frowns are not the only way we shape our children's attitudes. They are watching our own attitudes as adults, as parents—attitudes toward them, and attitudes toward our own problems. What was the last crisis you faced? What attitude did you exhibit before your children? Did you complain about the other person, how circumstances were against you, how life was unfair to you? If you did, would you be surprised to hear your child complain about an unfair teacher, an unfair test, or a bad school situation? How often we see ourselves projected through our children!

Here's an experiment for each of us. The next time we see a bad attitude in a child, ask if we have shown that same bad attitude during the last two weeks. Has our talk to our child been an attitude that is a beatitude, or a self-destructive attitude?

Attitudes are seeds, ready to hatch into actions, or ready to keep actions from hatching. A hostile attitude toward our neighbor may cause us to gossip to another neighbor about that person (action). Or that same hostile attitude may keep us from inviting the neighbor to church (lack of action). Our children perceive that hostile attitude. When a friend wrongs them, they will think it's okay to have a hostile attitude toward their friend. It's okay for my parents, so why not for me? So they may hatch their hostile attitude into unkind comments about this friend to others at school or may refuse to invite that friend to a birthday party or to Sunday school.

Do you know anyone whose parents sowed "can't" seeds in their children? "You can't do that," they often said. "You don't know how to do that. You're not big enough, or smart enough, or tough enough, or something enough." The seeds of the *fear* of failure grew into failure itself. These were not even seeds of actual failure, only the seeds of the *fear* of failure. Catch yourself if you are sowing "can't" seeds in your children. They are like thistle seeds planted in a fertile young life, someday springing up to choke out a young adult of promise. How do we sow these seeds? By our talk. By our attitudes toward our child. By continually reminding a child that he is dumb, or she isn't as pretty as a sister, or he can't ever hope to play on a team, or she can't get an A in that course.

It's easy also to sow seeds of bitterness in our children when those seeds have been planted in our own lives. Perhaps a father lost a job and was unfairly treated. The employer was bitter about circumstances and took it out on his employee, the child's father, sowing bitter seeds as he did. Seeds sown by an unfair employer take root in the children of the wronged person. The father simply passes those seeds of bitterness along to his children. How? By his talk. By his attitude. By what he says to his children about the employer, about his own state of mind, and even about God. In his bitterness the father may even come up with some new seeds of bitterness to sow in his child, "unfair" seeds, just like the unfair seeds his employer passed on to him.

I saw this happen in a cluster of churches during an economic downturn. Ten pastors were being forced from their churches, all in one mainline denomination and in one section of one state. Who was doing this? In each case, a small cluster of men who themselves had been forced from their jobs. They simply picked up the seeds dumped on them and planted them in their pastors. Is it possible that some of these pastors sowed these same seeds in their children?

Parents, watch carefully when seeds of bitterness are sown in your lives that you do not pass them on to your children! Guard your talk, so that you do not perpetuate a problem that has been dumped on you.

Here are some attitudes I hope I can pass on to my children and grandchildren. Would you like to pass these on too?

1) When I'm tempted to think "I can't do this," ask if I really can't. Is there another way to do it? If I really

can't, is there something just as important that I can do?

2) When I think something or someone is unfair, ask how I can become more fair to others because of what I have learned from this unfairness.

3) When I'm hurt because someone is against me, think of those who are for me.

4) When I'm tempted to feel sorry for myself, count my blessings.

5) When someone says an unkind word to me, think of something kind I can honestly say to that person.

6) When I fear that I will fail, think of three things that I have going for me that could help me succeed.

7) When I'm tempted to think "You don't love me anymore," ask what three specific acts of kindness you have shown me in the last week.

You can extend the list. The attitude you pass on to your child will be reflected in the attitude you show toward these and other circumstances. Your child too often becomes your attitude mirror, reflecting how you have responded to life's problems.

In summary, here are some guidelines to help us communicate attitudes that are beatitudes to our child:

1) We can respond to the same situation with opposite attitudes. The way we respond is up to us.

2) Our attitudes toward others are often reflected back to us, even from our children.

3) Our attitudes help determine our actions, so when we catch ourselves doing something wrong, it's time to check up on our attitudes that may have prompted that wrongdoing.

4) When we see bad attitudes in our children, we should first ask if we showed these same attitudes to them lately.

5) We should consciously ask what attitudes we want to communicate to our children, then seek to cultivate those attitudes in ourselves.

6) Check up on your conversation with your children. Each time you talk with a child today, ask what attitude you are projecting.

10

Are You Really FOR Your Child?

Are you really *for* your child? It sounds almost silly to ask a question like that. "Of course I'm for my child," you will answer.

Perhaps. But does your child know that? What do you think your child would say if a playmate or other peer would ask, "What makes you think your parents are on your side?"

The other night I watched a TV program, something I almost never do, mostly because there usually isn't much worth watching. This was a story about the Revolutionary War, a subject that I find interesting.

I watched with anger as the main character, a young man almost 16, was constantly put down by his father. The father belittled his thinking, made him feel like he was a child, told him that his mind had to catch up to his body, and in numerous ways let his son know that he really wasn't *for* him. That was certainly the message the son picked up until he overheard his mother and father talking one evening. He was amazed to hear his father say how much he loved "that boy" but it wasn't manly for a father to tell a son that he loved him.

That did it! I wanted to climb into the TV set and tell that misguided man that God the Father didn't think it was wrong to tell us, His sons and daughters, how much He loves us. Indeed, that is the transcending message of the Bible. Remove God's forthright proclamation of love from the Bible and the heart is gone.

Is God *for* you? Listen to these promises:

1) "I am with you and will watch over you wherever you go" (Genesis 28:15).

2) "I am he who comforts you" (Isaiah 51:12).

3) "The Lord your God is the one who goes with you to fight for you . . . to give you victory" (Deuteronomy 20:4).

4) "The Lord takes delight in his people" (Psalm 149:4).

5) "How great is the love the Father has lavished on us, that we should be called children of God!" (1 John 3:1).

6) "I will forgive their wickedness and will remember their sins no more" (Jeremiah 31:34).

7) "His ears are attentive to their cry" (Psalm 34:15).

Do those statements sound like God is too macho to say, "I love you and I am with you"?

Let's restate these five promises in simple, everyday language that we all understand:

1) I'm with you.

2) I'll comfort you.

3) I'll help you win.

4) I'm so pleased with you.

5) I love you.

6) I forgive you.

7) I'll listen to you.

There are dozens of other statements like these, assurances of God's love and care for us. Perhaps there are hundreds.

But let's start with these seven. If you frequently assured your child with one of these seven, what effect do you think it would have on your parent-child relationship?

May I ask an embarrassing question? When was the last time you said one of these assuring statements to your child? If God tells us, His children, repeatedly how much He loves us and how much He is for us, is it possible that we might discover a quality of godliness by communicating these truths to our children?

What would happen to the divorce rate in this country if husbands or wives did that? What if a husband put his arm around his wife each time she hurt and said, "I just want you to know that I'm with you; you can count on me"? What if a wife put her arm around her husband each time he was down and said, "Just remember, you can count on me"?

How many runaways would have stayed home if at least one parent had said "I'll listen to you; you can tell me anything and I'll put aside everything I'm doing to listen to you"?

Let's talk about seven scenarios with your child:

1) Your daughter comes home from school and you ask, "How was school today?" "Terrible," she replies. "Mary ignored me, Betty laughed at me, and Jody made fun of me. Everyone is against me." Option 1: You ignore what she said. Option 2: You tell her that her attitude has been bad at home and maybe that's why her friends are against her at school. Option 3: You say to your daughter, "I'm with you!" Which option would bond you more to your daughter, build a better lasting relationship with her? Which option reminds you of a promise from God?

2) Your son runs into the house crying. His friend has just picked on him and he feels deeply hurt. Option 1: You ignore him. Option 2: You tell him not to be

such a crybaby. Option 3: You say, "Come to me, let me comfort you." Which option reminds you of a promise of God? I realize as I say this that you can't rush to your child every time he cries and smother him with comfort. But he does need to know that when times are tough, you are there, as God is there, to comfort.

3) Your son is down because his friends toss a ball better than he does. Or your daughter is having trouble with a paper she has to write. Option 1: You ignore your child. Option 2: You say, "Why tell me? I always tossed a ball well," or, "I never had trouble writing papers." Option 3: You say, "I'll help you win. I'll help you learn to toss a ball better. I'll help you get going on your paper." Which option reminds you of a promise from God?

4) Your daughter comes home from school, bubbling with excitement. She has just been chosen for a key part in the school play, or she has just made a B in math even though math is not "her thing." Option 1: You ignore her. Option 2: You remind her that you had the lead part in your school play or you tell her that she could have made an A if she had worked harder. Option 3: You say, "I'm so pleased with you." Which option reminds you of a promise from God?

5) Some of your son's neighborhood playmates aren't all you wish they would be. You're a bit worried about your son caving in to peer pressure. Option 1: You ignore the situation. Option 2: You keep reminding your son to "stay on the straight and narrow." Option 3: You remind your son each day, "I love you. I'm for you. I'll help you know what is best for you. Then I'll trust you to please God and family. If you ever want to talk about anything, I'm here." Which option reminds you of a promise from God?

6) Your daughter gets into an argument with you one day and says some nasty things to you. Later she regrets what she has done and asks you to forgive her. Option 1: You ignore her, giving her the silent treatment. Option 2: You say equally nasty things to her about the nasty things she said to you. Option 3: You say, "I know you didn't mean to say those things, and I'm sure you won't say those things again. I forgive you." Which option reminds you of a promise from God?

7) Your son runs into the house with some important news about a friend. He starts to tell you, but you have just started to get dinner, or you're in the middle of your favorite TV program. Option 1: You keep on with dinner or the TV program. Option 2: You scold him for interrupting and tell him not to do that again. Option 3: You decide that dinner or TV can do without you, but your son can't. So you tell your son, "I'm listening. Tell me what's on your heart." Which option reminds you of a promise from God?

In each of these seven scenarios, do you notice a common thread? The third options are modern paraphrases of the seven Bible promises. Can we say that these are the Godlike options, the godly options, because they are like the promises God has made to us? I think so.

Jesus said that if we are not for Him, we are against Him (Matthew 12:30). Would it surprise you to know that your child thinks that too?

The Golden Rule may help you and me understand how much our child wants us to be for him. Perhaps we could restate the Golden Rule like this: "I should decide how I want others to treat me. Then I should first treat others that way."

Ask yourself how you want your husband or wife or child to treat you. Do you want them to be *for* you, truly for you? I suspect you do. If so, then you should lead the way by being *for* your mate or child. Lead the way in what you say to them each day and you will be surprised to see how much they become for you.

I can't prove this, but I think we would eliminate most divorce, parent-child conflict, and family tension if we could truly be *for* each other in the home.

When I am for my child, I want to see my child succeed, I want to see my child happy and fulfilled, I want to see my child develop a healthy self-image, I want my child to develop a healthy relationship with other people and with God, and I want my child to develop a productive, redemptive life. When I am for my child, my conversation with my child will become bricks and mortar to help build the kind of life that will please God and give the child a rewarding life.

Think of someone you believe has truly been for you. How did you know that? What does this person do for you that others don't? How does this person talk with you that others don't?

I want my children to know that I am truly for them. When a troubled day comes along and it seems that the whole world is against them, I want them to know there is always a refuge where they will find a mother and father for them. That is the biblical picture of God also, isn't it? This is one of the ways I hope to be godly, to be like God. In summary, here are some questions to ask to help you assess if you are *for* your child as God is *for* you:

1) If your child is talking with a friend, do you think he would say, "My parents are on my side; no matter what happens, I can count on them to want the best for me"?

2) If your child is talking with a friend, do you think she would say, "When something is wrong and I feel

hurt, I go to my parents first because they help me feel better"?

3) If your child is talking with a friend, do you think he would say, "I can count on my parents to want the best for me; they really want me to do what will help me most"?

4) If your child is talking with a friend, do you think she would say, "Whenever I do my best, even if it's not all my parents want, they say how pleased they are with what I have done"?

5) If your child is talking with a friend, do you think he would say, "My parents really love me, even when I don't deserve it"?

6) If your child is talking with a friend, do you think she would say, "I can count on my parents to forgive me when I'm really sorry for something stupid I've done"?

7) If your child is talking with a friend, do you think he would say, "My parents are good listeners; when I want to talk, they want to listen"?

11

Talking So Children WANT to Listen

It was a sizzling hot July morning in Washington D.C. when I crawled into the van with my son Ron, his wife Becki, and little Jason and Amy. I was dog-tired after four days of interviews and meetings at the Christian Bookseller's Association annual convention. I welcomed a quiet drive to the Adirondack Mountains, where my wife Arlie would join us for a much-needed vacation.

"Sorry about the air conditioner," Ron greeted me. "It went out on us." We had ten hours of driving ahead with five of us in the van, lots of luggage, and the temperature in the 90's.

At a time like this we usually don't want to talk with anyone. We would rather crawl into a hole and swelter in silence. Then I saw two little faces, with smiles as broad as the sunshine, waiting for Grandpa to crawl into the van with them. They couldn't wait to tell me all about their adventures in Washington.

It was tempting for Ron and me to start talking about the convention, comparing notes and giving reactions. We had gone our separate ways at the convention, and this was our first opportunity to reflect on what we had seen.

But it was obvious that convention talk would have to wait. There were much more important things to talk about.

Two-year-old Jason had new shoes, and at that moment they were the most important things in the whole world to him. He had to tell his grandpa about them, and of course I had a dozen questions for him. Where did he get them? What color were they? How did he like them? Who tied his shoestrings for him? And so on.

Four-year-old Amy had a much wider assortment of things to talk about—her visit to her uncle's and aunt's home, afternoon at the museum, and a postcard of the ruby slippers of The Wizard of Oz fame. She had actually seen the ruby slippers at the museum in Washington. Honestly!

I think Ron and I never did get to talk about the convention. The ten hours slipped by with great delight as we talked of ruby slippers, new shoes, museum visits, and a hundred other concerns that filled the hearts and minds of two little children. At last Amy put her head on Grandpa's shoulder and fell asleep, assured that her concerns were truly important—so important that we had made them our highest priority.

I look back on that day with delight, a time of further bonding with two VIP's. I'm so glad that Ron and I never started to talk about the convention. Ruby slippers, a little boy's shoes, and a visit to an aunt and uncle may not seem as important as a national convention, but they are much more important to the Amys and Jasons of our families—and aren't the Amys and

Jasons of our families much more important than our conventions and businesses?

Did these children *want* to listen to their parents and me talk? Of course they did, because we were talking about their interests, their concerns. Would they have listened if we had talked about the convention? Perhaps for a minute or two at the most. Then they would have retreated into toys or books in their own private little corner. And I would have lost a most wonderful opportunity to interact with my little VIP's and lay up another brick or two in our growing lifelong relationship.

We may think we are different from a two-year-old or a four-year-old, and in some ways we are. But like them, we want to talk about our concerns, our interests, ourselves. And so do your children.

Do you ever sit down with your child and talk for a few minutes about his or her concerns only? Finding a few minutes each day to do this will pay handsome dividends in building a relationship of loving trust with your child.

What will you talk about? What is your child concerned about most? What did she do at school today? Who does he like best at school? Is there a special friend? What do this friend and your child like to do together?

People who are good conversationalists will tell you that you can talk for hours with anyone of any age, at any intellectual level, adult or child, and hold them captivated. All you have to do is show a genuine interest in that person and ask questions that help you explore that interest. What does this person do? How does he do it? What does she like? Why?

Reflect back on the last three conversations you have had with someone. Did that person show a genuine interest in how you spend your day, what you like or don't like, what you think about certain matters, and what you would do if you were in a certain situation? I think it's safe to say that you have had very few persons ask you questions like these about your thoughts, your concerns, your convictions, your values, your interests, your reactions, your "heartbeat" about life. Most of us can count these kinds of conversations on the fingers of one hand and have fingers left over.

If you want people to show this loving concern for your interests, think how much more your child wants you, as parent, the most important person in the world to him, to show that loving concern for his interests.

Talking about the other person's concerns acknowledges his personhood, turns the spotlight of your attentive love upon his personhood, and starts a small celebration to honor it. On that hot July day in the van, I put Amy and Jason on the stage, in the direct beam of the spotlight of my attention, then struck up the orchestra and held a full-fledged party to honor them as VIP's.

If you meet me sometime, humor me by asking me a dozen questions about this book. Why did I write it? What kind of talking relationship have I had with my own children? My grandchildren? What was the toughest problem I have encountered in talking with little children? You can come up with eight more. But be genuinely interested in answers or don't ask the questions.

Better still, ask me a dozen questions about me. Put me on the center of your life's stage for a few moments to show that you care. I'll become your friend, especially when I recognize that you sincerely want to ask those dozen questions and are not doing it because I asked you to do it here.

As your children grow up, find those special times to put them in the center of your spotlight of interest.

Give them a hero party in your conversation, even for a few minutes each day.

When we set aside a few minutes each day with each child to genuinely explore his concerns, you honor that child as surely as the Academy of Motion Picture Arts and Sciences honors a star with an Oscar. Your attentive interest in talking with your child about his concerns is as important to him as an awards banquet—and in a sense it *is* a daily awards banquet in his honor. It's your way of giving him an Oscar each day. Actually it's better than an Oscar because it's a person-to-person honor without any hint of politics.

But exactly what should you say when you take those few precious moments to talk with your child? That depends on what your child has just done. Did he just come home from school? Is it time to read her a bedtime story? Did he just break a favorite dish? Is she having a temper tantrum? Is he sassing you back about something? Did she just come through the door crying because some friends mistreated her?

Start with the circumstance. That's always a good starting point because that is uppermost in the child's mind at that time. Then go from there.

But don't start the adventure of asking about the child's interests and then abandon the conversation as soon as you start. Have you ever had people do this to you? A friend asks, "What are you doing these days?" You have so much to tell, but after a sentence or two your friend is off on a totally different subject. Don't do this with your child; follow through on the conversation.

Suppose your child comes home from school and you ask, "How was school today?" (a good generic question). Your child answers "Terrible!" or "Great!" This is no time to bail out of the conversation. Hidden in those two words are bundles of feelings and problems and reactions and concerns that need to be talked through. "Why was it terrible?" (or great). "What happened?" "Could you have done anything to prevent this problem?" "How could you keep this from happening tomorrow?" Keep asking questions until your child is ready to stop or until you think you have reached an optimum point in your talk.

What questions do you ask your child? What do you say to this young VIP?

Arlie and I reflected on our conversations with our children when they were younger. Here are a few questions we think we asked from time to time. Some of them relate to coming home from school, some are breakfast questions, some are dinner questions, some are bedtime questions, and some are questions relating to times of hurting:

1) Is there something special you want to do for a friend today? Is there something special you would like to do with me for a few minutes when you come home from school?

2) Who do you like best in your school? What do you like best about this person?

3) What did your teacher (or friends) say about your new dress today (shoes, shirt, whatever)?

4) Did someone make you especially happy (or angry) today? What happened? How did you feel about this?

5) How was school today? This is a generic question, but sometimes these are good to bring out things you never guessed your child was thinking.

6) Who did you like best in the story I read tonight? Do you know anyone like (this character)? How is this person like him? What would you like to say to this character about the way she behaved?

7) Are you ever sad? (or happy, or angry, or any other emotion or feeling). What made you sad? What did you do about it? How did that help you not feel sad anymore?

8) What do you like best about your Sunday school class? Is there anything you don't like about it?

9) What's your favorite game? Your favorite toy? Why do you like this game or toy so much?

10) What did you like best about the TV program we just watched? What did you think these people did that was wrong? Why?

I could continue on for dozens of pages with hypothetical questions. You will notice that these questions focus on what the child is thinking or feeling about life rather than what you or someone else is thinking or feeling.

How can you talk so that your child will *want* to listen and want to talk with you? Talk about concerns of your child's heart. That's true for any of us, isn't it?

Exploring your child's heart and mind is one of life's great adventures. Exploring that young mind is more exhilarating than exploring new lands. It is part of the great adventure of living. Once you form the habit, you will not want to break it. But you must set out to make this a daily, conscious habit or the days will slip by without cultivating talk that makes your child *want* to listen.

In summary, here are some guidelines concerning talking so that your child will want to listen:

1) Your children, like us, want to listen when we talk about their concerns.

2) When we talk about our children's concerns, we must be genuinely interested in the adventure of exploring their interests with them.

3) Talk through the various "layers" of interest. Don't ask a leading question, such as "How was school

today?" unless you are willing to ask another question when your child replies "Terrible!"

4) Find some time each day, even a few minutes, when you genuinely talk with your child about his concerns. Make this a habit, a practice. Sometimes you will do it at breakfast, or lunch, or snacktime, or dinner, or bedtime, or times when your child comes through the door crying. If you make this a high priority, you will find time to do it because you will put this ahead of some things of lesser importance.

12

Parents Should Listen Too!

"Dad, you're not listening to me!" I'm not sure which of my five children said that, but I think it was perhaps each of them at one time or another. It's easy to get engros ed in a newspaper or book or TV program or any one of a dozen distractions. A small voice comes at you obliquely in the background, only to be drowned in our preoccupation in the immediate, absorbed in the soft cushion of our cultivated attention process that tunes out all but what we want to hear.

People who live near busy highways or railways learn to tune out unwanted noise. I've worked in offices where the distraction level was relatively high, but after a period of time I learned to tune out everything except my immediate work.

We even learn to respond to something we've tuned out without realizing we have responded to it. Your child comes into the room while you're reading the newspaper. "Dad, can I have a hundred dollars?" the child asks.

Don't be surprised if you say okay without even

thinking. (Also don't be surprised if your child is surprised!)

I've been guilty of this, and I suspect you have too. We have trained ourselves to selectively focus on the immediate. All else is an unwanted distraction that infringes on that focused attention.

Why does immediacy prevail? We consistently put secondary immediacy above primary importance. For example, while you are doing something you consider of prime importance, the phone rings. It may be a total stranger trying to sell aluminum siding, or a wrong number. But the ringing phone will prevail. We have conditioned ourselves to put the immediacy of a ringing phone above something far more important.

Or perhaps you are doing something important when the doorbell rings. What prevails? The doorbell, every time. We have conditioned our minds to set ringing bells above heart-to-heart talks, important work, devotions, personal reflection, or a dozen other important activities. Ringing bells are almost always at the top of the priority list. It's crazy, isn't it, because it usually puts total strangers above those we love most, merely because the total stranger is in control of the ringing bell. Then we're angry when we realize that the aluminum-siding salesman has captured our priorities at a sensitive moment.

How we listen is conditioned by how we respond to outside stimuli. Somehow I don't listen as well when Arlie says, "Honey, someone needs to take out the garbage" as I do when she says, "Honey, it's time for dinner." Garbage doesn't rank as high in my attentiveness as dinner.

A blaring car horn captures my attention faster than a soft voice that calls from a car window, "I think you're walking in the path of my speeding car, sir."

That's probably why automakers put horns on cars rather than soft voices.

If you want to know what makes people listen, watch TV commercials. The admakers are masters of the art of making you listen (and watch). Sometimes it's more interesting to watch the commercials and skip the program. Admakers don't reason with you about all the wonderful features of a product. They try to capture your attention by tossing at you one delight-ful (or seductive) benefit that you will receive if you use their product, and they do it in a way that is so unique that you can't forget what was said.

But there is a fundamental difference between the purpose of the admaker and that of the parent. A good admaker is trying get you to listen so you will buy a product. A good parent is trying to listen so he can build a person. A good admaker wants you to listen so he can get something from you. A good parent wants to listen so he can give something to his child.

Since admakers and parents start with radically different purposes, we need to assess their desire for listening and our desire as parents for listening in a radically different light. But while we do it, we should learn from them.

Admakers, at least through their commercials, can-not afford to be listeners. Parents, on the other hand, cannot afford *not* to be listeners. Admakers are di-recting their communication, not to a million unique individuals, but to a million generic persons rep-resenting a wide cross-section of listeners. Parents usually direct their communication to a very unique person and customize their communication to that specific person and his needs. No TV commercial can do that. No TV commercial can listen attentively and lovingly while your child cries about his hurt finger.

So if you want to understand the devices that in-duce listening, study commercials. If you want to create the art of *being* a good listener, do *not* listen to commercials but cultivate this art with that wonder-fully unique person who holds a most high priority in your life—your child.

My son-in-law Kevin Engel is the discipleship youth director in a large church and works with almost 200 young people and their leaders in the area of disciple-ship. He tells me that one of their keynote phrases for youth leaders and parents is "If you want kids to listen to you, it's better to have good questions than good answers."

We talked about this today. Another way to say this would be "It's better to have good questions before you try to give good answers." You can't truly offer solutions until you understand problems, and you can't truly understand your child's problems until you listen carefully to your child verbalize those problems. Sometimes listening is much more helpful to your child than talking. It's a good policy to always listen before talking. And good listening requires good questions. Asking questions and listening are insep-arable.

Some of you who are parents of teens will say, "But my teen turns me off when I ask questions. He thinks I'm too nosy. She thinks I'm prying or checking up on her. He thinks it's a sign I don't trust him."

Kevin and I think such responses may flag two problems. First, you really need to start asking ques-tions and listening from the earliest years. If you are a parent of a young child, start now; don't wait. Start as early in life as possible to ask questions and to listen. If you suddenly start to ask questions when your child is a teen, and you haven't done much of this before, it's likely that he will think you're nosy or she will think you're prying.

The second problem may be the attitude you bring to your questions for your teen child. Are you really prying? Are you really nosy? Or are you genuinely interested in what your child has to say, even if you may not agree with all of it? Check up on your motives and make sure your questions and your listening are not for *your* benefit (curiosity, nosiness, etc.) but for *your child's* benefit: to cultivate you as a parental friend and guide.

A third problem may be the way you have responded in the past. If your child has consistently sent signals that you are nosy, it's time to ask what signals you sent as you responded to the little differences you and your child have had. Have you given your child some margin to be different without shaming him? Have you "flown off the handle" when you heard your child express something you don't like? If you consistently make it hard for your child to confide in you, he won't!

Bad parental attitudes easily sneak upon us. It's easy to say things like "Why do you always argue with me?" or "Why do you always listen to your friends but not to me?" or "You love your friends more than me because you spend more time with them." Two little words are killers: "always" and "never." Children and parents throw these at each other as though they are having food fights with them. "You never clean up your room." "You always argue with me." "You never want to please me." "You always think you're so smart."

A good listener is first and foremost a good question-asker. (We'll talk more about questions in the next chapter.) Good listeners don't sit there like bumps on logs and expect the other person, especially a child, to initiate and carry on all the talk. Cultivate the art of asking caring questions. Then cultivate the art of asking follow-up questions.

It's easy to think of talking as active and listening as passive, but good listening is at least as active as good talking. Good listening is a cultivated art. That's why you and your child need to cultivate this art together throughout the growing-up years.

The foundation of good listening is what I think of you. What you say is important to me because first and foremost you are important to me. Again, this is an attitude that must be cultivated from earliest childhood. I've mentioned elsewhere in this book that Arlie and I viewed our children at birth as 1) a full person, not a little blob that would grow to become a person, and 2) equal to us in God's eyes.

If you start with these two assumptions, you will take an entirely different approach in child development than if you assume your child is much less of a person than you. You will cultivate a lasting friendship with your child and your child will accept you not only as his parent but in a sense as his peer—and that's a strong basis for friendship.

If I recognize that my child is one of the most important people in my life, I will want to listen. I will put listening to my child at the top of the priority list. I will try to put down my newspaper, or postpone setting the table, or delay whatever I'm doing in order to listen to my child's concerns. (Obviously your child has to learn that he doesn't always have the floor with petty things while you're busy.)

Listening to my child is celebrating his personhood, recognizing the value of him as a person. Listening to my child is my way of saying "You are important to me. I really want to know what you are thinking, what you are doing, how you are responding to life, and how I can help you cope with the things that are delighting you or bothering you."

Listening to my child is my way of throwing a hero party for her, striking up the band and playing "Hail to the Chief" for him, awarding her an Oscar for a starring role in my life. When my child talks and I don't listen, or I'm listening with one ear but it's all going out the other ear, I'm telling him loud and clear that he is not important to me because what he says is not important to me.

Check up on yourself and ask what kind of listener you are when your child talks to you. That may be highly revealing about what attitude you have toward the value of your child in your life. You may discover your priority system and where your child fits into that system.

Too many Christian parents participate in youth seminars because they did not listen to their children when they were younger. Now at the eleventh hour, when problems become more highly visible in a child's life, they are scrambling to put the pieces together again. Please, please—cultivate the art of listening to your young child so that your VIP will want to listen to you as a teen!

Should your child listen to you, the parent? Of course. Listening is a two-way street. But this chapter is about the parent as listener. The child as listener was the subject of the previous chapter.

In summary, here are some questions to help you determine if you are a good listener to your child:

1) Do I let immediacy, the urgent things of lesser importance, assume priority over listening to my child?

2) Like a TV commercial, do I sometimes content myself with getting my child's attention and selling

him my point of view rather than meeting his need to have a parental listener?

3) When I ask my child questions, do I expect the answers to satisfy my own curiosity or nosiness or do I genuinely want to be a good listener?

4) Do I think that what my child says is important because I think my child is important?

5) Do I consider my role as parent to merely keep my child on the straight and narrow, or instead to help my child grow as the kind of person who will please God? Am I truly celebrating my child's personhood when I ask questions and listen?

13

Talking Is Asking

"But what should I say?" Mary asks. Mary is worried because she and her husband will join an important client and his wife for dinner tonight. But what should she talk about? How can she help to carry on a conversation with two important strangers for the entire evening?

Have you ever been in Mary's predicament? You're going to spend a few minutes, or a few hours, with someone important. What do you say? What do you talk about? It's enough to make you a nervous wreck. You want to be a good conversationalist, but you don't have the gift of gab as some friends do.

Here's a secret that many people have never learned: The gift of gab does not make a person a good conversationalist, and in fact it sometimes makes a person a domineering bore. Have you ever spent the evening with someone who talks incessantly but says nothing, or someone who talks incessantly but asks nothing? You can become a great conversationalist even if you do not have the gift of gab. Plain ordinary people like you and me can easily become great conversationalists. How?

It's no secret that you can be a stunning conversationalist if you learn the art of *asking questions*. You never have to worry about what to *say* if you know what to *ask*. That's because people are much more interested in talking about themselves than in talking about a subject.

But why? Do we want to talk about ourselves to satisfy our ego, or is there something more significant here than ego satisfaction?

When I ask you a genuine question about your thoughts, your feelings, your work, your attitudes, your experiences, or anything else that concerns you, I extend a person-to-person invitation. I as a person show a genuine interest in you as a person. My personhood reaches out to your personhood, asking that your personhood responds to my personhood. We have each transcended the raw practical world of subject matter and have entered into the exciting adventure of personhood. Remove personhood from heaven or earth and either becomes a sterile test tube devoid of love, grace, truth, peace, friendship, and a hundred other qualities that make life exciting because it is personal.

A question is one of the most wonderful communications devices in the world. Few elements of our language are so effective in bringing our personhoods into harmony as a genuine question about you. A question may, of course, transact business on a subject level. But at its best, it rises above mere subject matter to reach deeply into personal heartbeat. I know of no other communications device so effective in helping you or me to walk with sensitivity into one another's lives. What would our lives be without simple questions?

It's unlikely that anyone will ever fall in love without asking questions. It's almost certain that no one will get married without asking questions, especially *the* question. Beyond that, the right questions keep marriage and parent-child relationships alive. They build our personal interest in and concern for one another.

Parent and child grow through the years into that "best friend" relationship when the parent frequently asks warm, wonderful questions that help the child respond to the essence of parental personhood and present in return the essence of childhood personhood. Questions that parents and children ask each other can be strong bonds of exploration and affirmation of one another. They tell one another, "I care about you—what you think, how you feel, what you want to do or don't want to do, and a hundred other things."

Not all questions that parents ask are so wonderful, of course. There are mean-spirited questions that reach into one another's personhood like sandpaper, abrasive and irritating: "Why did you do such a stupid thing?" "What were you thinking about when you said that?" "How can you be so dumb?" "Who do you think you are, anyway?" Questions like these certainly do not affirm personhood or explore personhood with a loving spirit of friendship. I would call these demeaning questions, designed to make ourselves look bigger by making the other person look smaller.

There are judgmental questions, too: "What do you think God would like to do to you right now?" "Don't you think God will get you for this?" "How can you live with yourself after that?" In effect, these are really not questions at all but are statements of judgment. The questioner is saying, "God is going to get you"; "He's going to punish you"; "You won't be able to live with yourself." We are judging the other person with a statement phrased as a question. There is not much affirmation or building of friendship here.

Then there are cross-examination questions, like the kind an attorney would ask in a murder trial. "Where were you on the way home?" "What were you doing in your room with the door closed?" "What did your friend say to you when you were behind the house?" I know you're guilty and I'm going to pry it out of you. Confess up!

Of course there are times when our questions need to be forthright so we can unmask a deception. If we must, we must. It's part of our role as parental shepherds. But even those times can be handled with grace and a loving spirit. There is never an appropriate time for a parent to ask mean-spirited or demeaning questions. Never!

If we make cross-examination the mission of our parenting, or make a habit of passing judgment through questions, we will destroy parent-child relationships. We will create in the minds of our children a nagging feeling that we do not trust them and that we are always behind the next bush spying on them.

Looking back over 35 years of parenting, with strong parent-child relationships that have endured through the years, I believe the spirit of trust has perhaps been the strongest glue that has bound us together. Isn't a spirit of trust the strong glue that binds most of our important relationships together? What would happen to your marriage if your mate each day communicated to you a lack of trust? Before long you would wonder if you even trust yourself.

Imagine that you are a growing child again. If your parents affirm you often as a person whom they *can* trust and *do* trust, you will want to live up to that trust. But if you are constantly told, through statements or questions, that you are a bad boy or a bad girl, you will soon begin to fulfill their prophecy.

I believe that one of our truly important parental missions is to build our children into strong persons, and especially strong godly persons. Much of this is accomplished through questions that reach our personhood into theirs so that they may reciprocate and reach their personhood into ours.

The seven interrogatives are the seven foundation stones upon which all questions are laid: who, when, why, what, which, how, and where. Not all questions use these exact words, but in essence almost all questions seek to get at one of these root ideas.

Most of our simple, everyday questions use one of the seven interrogatives. "How do you like your new dress?" "When would you like to go to the zoo?" "What would you like to do this afternoon?" "Who is your favorite person in this book?" "Why do you think this person said what he did?" "Where would you like to go on vacation?" "Which pair of shoes do you like better?"

In each of these questions we are asking a child to express preferences, values, likes or dislikes, convictions, or choices in order to bring personhood to bear on the decision-making process. Growth is the determination of the paths that our personhood will follow, fostered by learning to make the right choices or decisions. Growth is a day-by-day, brick-by-brick, nail-by-nail, question-by-question, answer-by-answer process. Growth says, "I will be a little higher up the mountainside tomorrow because I have chosen the right road to take me there."

What you say or ask your child is merely a fulfillment of what you want your child to become. Have you decided what kind of person you want your child to be? A leader? A man of God? A woman of God? A thoughtful decision-maker? Someone who has learned to make the right choices? Someone who is honest with herself? Someone who knows how to discipline himself? Do you want him to exhibit Christian graces? Do you want her life to be built on Christian values such as truthfulness, thankfulness, kindness, and more?

If your parental mission is to build your child as a strong person, a leader, a man or woman of God, your questions, like your conversations, will tend to be building blocks that help your child grow to be that strong person, that leader, that man or woman of God.

Judgmental questions, demeaning questions, cross-examination questions do not build. They tear down. They rob your child of legitimate personal dignity.

What type of questions build? Those that help our child grow to become a stronger person, especially the kind of person whom God desires. Here are some types of building questions:

1) Questions that help us learn to make good choices or decisions.

A simple question such as "Which shoes do you like best?" lays a foundation stone for decision-making. It says to the child, "Your choice is important; you must learn what is good or bad, better or best."

It's much easier, of course, for you as a parent to walk into the shoe store with your child and say, "You don't know what's best for you, so I'll choose your shoes for you." Perhaps a young child *doesn't* know what is best for him. But it's our job as parents to help him learn what is best for him.

What if your child says, "I like these shoes best," and you are convinced that he has made a bad decision? What should you do now?

The easiest response is to say, "That's a bad decision; try again," or, "That's a bad choice; I knew I should make the decision for you."

Your child will likely trust you and will let you make the decision (he doesn't have a choice!), but you're not helping him learn to decide.

A better approach is to ask some other questions that help the child understand the consequences of his choice. Let's pretend:

"Which shoes do you like best?"

"These! Everyone is wearing these" (child points to purple shoes).

"Those are interesting. Do you like purple?"

"Yeah!"

"We can afford to get you only one pair this fall. Do you think you will like purple next month and the next?"

"Sure!"

"How do you think those will look with your red shirt?"

"I don't know."

"What will you think if your friends stop wearing purple next month? Will you still wear them?"

Silence.

"Is there another color you like almost as much as purple, but you'll still like next month and the next?"

I don't know if purple is in or out this month. But the point is that it's better to explore with your child some factors that may affect his choice later, or when trends change, or when friends change. Let's look at another scenario.

"Which shoes do you like best?"

"These!" (child points to purple shoes).

"Purple! You won't like those things in another month. I know you won't. Then you'll come begging me to buy you another pair of shoes, and we can't afford it." That settles the whole matter. You've told your child that he has made a dumb decision and you will take over now.

My plea is not how you unsell your child when he wants purple shoes (you may have some very different questions from mine), but how you help your child think about consequences when he makes a bad decision. At some age he must learn to live with consequences. One of the most common reasons that people fail is not incompetence but a lack of accountability.

As a parent, you can't smother your child for life. You won't be there when he decides who he wants to date, or when she is confronted with the temptation of premarital sex. You won't decide for your child who to marry and whether or not that is a dumb decision. You probably won't decide many important decisions that he or she will make as a late teen. There are hundreds of decisions a teen will make without you there to help decide what is best. You'd better help your child learn to choose now!

When parents help younger children learn about consequences and accountability through concerned and loving questions, their teen later will remember this decision-making process when he is faced with monumental decisions, such as who to marry.

2) Questions that bond our child while freeing him.

When is the right time to cut the cord that ties the child to the parent? Some think this happens when a child gets married. Others think it happens when a child leaves home to get a job or go to college. Still others think this happens at a certain age.

None of these is correct. Binding our child to us and loosening the child from us are simultaneous. The day our child is born we begin to bind him, or bond her, to us in a spirit of trust and loyalty, love and friendship, care and share. But on that same day we begin the monumental job of helping our child to be independent, self-sustaining, to make it on his own. We teach our children to tie shoes, go to the bathroom, dress, eat, and dozens of other self-sustaining activities.

So through our questions we are in the business of bonding and freeing at the same time. Isn't that also what God does with His children? While He bonds us to Him personally, He frees us to make our own decisions and to live with the consequences. Bonding is person-to-person, merging two persons for the mutual growth and benefit that each brings to the other. Freeing is person-to-person, releasing two persons for the mutual growth and benefit that each brings to the other.

3) Questions that help us discover ourselves and our gifts during the growing formative years.

My friend Dick Hagstrom is a management consultant, in the business of helping executives (and other leaders) discover their gifts and how best to apply them. When I took Dick's test, I was amazed at the skill with which he walked quietly into my mind and heart and turned over rock after rock that I didn't even know was there in order to help me discover the real me. When we finished, and he applied his perceptive skills, I knew more about my personal gifts than I had ever known before.

Dick is a master of questions. His test is essentially question after question, both written and oral, to peel back the layers of our experience until we discover who we really are.

I think we need to package something for parents to help their children discover their personal gifts. If we do, it must be a package of skillful questions. These would certainly never be demeaning questions, or cross-examination questions, or judgmental questions. They would be loving, gentle, probing questions, not so much to give the parent answers as to help the child discover himself as he gives himself answers. Self probes self with questions to give self answers. Self answers self to discover self.

4) Questions that follow up previous questions—layers of questions.

This morning a friend called. "Hi, how are you?" I asked. "Fine," he answered. "How are you?" "Fine," I answered.

These are ritualistic questions. We don't expect more than ritualistic answers. What if, instead of saying "fine," my friend had said "terrible—never felt worse." What would I have said? The ritual would have been broken.

A couple of years after Arlie and I lost our son Doug, we met some friends who also lost their son. We had gone through parallel tragedies miles apart with two sons almost the same age.

"How are you two doing?" the lady asked. "Fine," we responded. That was the proper ritual, of course.

"No, I want to know how you are *really* doing," she asked. The ritual was broken. We talked about our pain. She and her husband talked of their pain. We explored one another's mind and heart and learned something of the meaning of loss.

I've gone through this ritual hundreds of times with people. So have you. I've gone through it hundreds of times with my children.

"How was school today?"

"Fine."

"That's good."

"How were things here at home today?"

"Fine."

"Good."

There's no probing of personhood at all. It's like two ducks meeting at the pond and quacking to each other.

We need to cultivate the art of asking layers of questions with our children, using follow-up questions that are genuine questions. The little ritual above is not made up of questions at all because we are not trying to get answers. Genuine questions seek genuine answers. Ritualistic questions seek ritualistic answers.

Let's try the ritual above in another way:

"How was school today?"

"Fine."

"That's good. What did you do that you liked best?"

Now you have something to talk about. Or you could have said, "That's good. Was there anything about school that you didn't like?" Or, "That's good. What did you do at recess this morning?" Or, "That's good. Was your teacher helpful today?"

There are dozens of follow-up questions you could ask to stop the ritual and move into genuine person-to-person talk.

Affirming answers before asking another question is often helpful. Let's take the same scenario:

"How was school today?"

"Fine."

"I'm glad to hear you say it's fine. That really makes me feel good when you're feeling good. What did you do at recess?"

Sometimes you may feel it helpful to rephrase the child's answer or turn it over a bit. Let's try the same scenario, except the day at school wasn't fine:

"How was school today?"

"Not so good."

"I'm sorry. Why wasn't it so good?"

Or you might answer, "Not so good? Do you mean only a little not-so-good or really and truly not-so-good?" Rephrasing helps to clarify what we might otherwise accept in the wrong way. We might think our child had a bad day when he is really responding to a friend who had a bad day.

"Oh, my day was okay, but I felt so sorry for Mary. She lost her father."

You might never have discovered that fact if you hadn't asked another layer of questions. Now you have opened the opportunity to talk with your child about her vicarious encounter with death.

Questions enrich our lives and our relationships. What would we do without this wonderful device to become guests in the inner sanctum of the other person's life?

What you ask and what you answer are important, not because your answers are so important but because *you* are important, and because when I ask, I communicate that fact to you. When I ask and listen, I celebrate you. I make you a true celebrity.

Looking back, I'm glad Arlie and I asked our children thousands of questions and they in turn asked us thousands of questions. Our children are grown now, but we still ask each other dozens of questions, almost every week.

We knock and enter the doorways of each other's lives hundreds of times each year. We seek their heartbeat and they seek ours. They ask for our insights and we share them. We seek to give them the gift of ourselves, and they reciprocate with the same gift to us.

The following words of Jesus are right on target for effective parent-child conversations through questions. "Ask and it will be given to you; seek and you will find; knock and the door will be opened to you. For everyone who asks receives; he who seeks finds; and to him who knocks, the door will be opened. Which of you, if his son asks for bread, will give him a stone? Or if he asks for a fish, will give him a snake? If you, then, though you are evil, know how to give good gifts to your children, how much more will your Father in heaven give good gifts to those who ask him! In everything, do to others what you would have them do to you, for this sums up the Law and the Prophets" (Matthew 7:7-12).

In summary, here are some guidelines for developing conversational skills in our children through questions:

1) A question is one of our most powerful communications devices to help us reach deeply into each other's lives.

2) Some questions demean, judge, or cross-examine our children, putting their self-image in jeopardy. Parents who practice asking these types of questions risk their parent-child relationships.

3) All questions are rooted in the seven interrogatives—who, when, why, what, which, how, and where. Use these generously and you will always have something to talk about with your children.

4) Our children grow as they, through questions, are confronted with choices, decisions, preferences, values, likes or dislikes, or convictions.

5) The questions we ask our children fulfill our expectations for our children.

6) Bonding our child to us and freeing our child from us are simultaneous parental functions, both accomplished well through questions.

7) Questions help our children discover themselves and their gifts.

8) Many questions are ritualistic, used for formalities. Cultivate layers of questions that follow up the "icebreaker" question and give the child an opportunity to reach into his mind and heart.

14

Talking Through Traditions

Someone said, "Actions speak louder than words." That's because *visibility* captures attention better than *audibility*. Visibility also leaves a more lasting impression than audibility. Think back on scenes of childhood. Try to remember three of the most impressionable scenes. What do you remember most—what you heard or what you saw? Unless it was a highly significant statement, or a particularly brutal statement, or an unusually loving statement, you will more than likely remember something you saw more than something you heard.

If this is true, then nonverbal communication with our children may even be more powerful and more lasting than verbal communication. What you do speaks so loudly that I can't hear what you say.

There's another statement that says, "Don't do as I do, do as I say." That's usually said in jest because most of us know that parenting doesn't work that way. Our children *will* do what we do more than what we say, not necessarily today, but at a later tomorrow.

Role-modeling is a most powerful means of communication. If I say to my children, "God is always there," but I'm never there with them, how can I expect them to believe what I say about God? Or if I say to my children, "God will always listen to your prayers," but I'm always so busy and involved that I can't take the time to listen to their small problems, what I say is nullified by what I do.

If I tell my children that God is love, but I am unloving, why should they listen? If I tell them that God is truth but they hear me bend the truth more than occasionally, why should they believe me? If I tell them that God is hope, but I am always living at the edge of despair, how can I get my message across to them? A life of parental impurity will cancel out all our little sermons about the holiness of God. A life of rancor and bitterness between husband and wife or parent and child will delete our statements about the lovingkindness of our heavenly Father.

Through the years I have become increasingly convinced that our parental conduct before our children does indeed speak much louder than all the speeches and sermonettes we give them. Daily living is indeed much more powerful than daily lecturing.

That's why I like family traditions so much—they are filled with role-modeling. Traditions capture a host of role-modeling adventures and wrap them into one marvelous package.

Family traditions provide parental role-modeling in many ways. Here are seven. Each is a distinct way of "talking" with your children about the matters that you consider important.

1) Family traditions speak of parental priorities.

In our family we have several traditions that are played out year after year. Birthdays are a big deal, and always have been. When children are home, or when we can celebrate that same week, there is a cake with candles plus gifts and singing. When children can't be home, there is always a telephone call with "Happy Birthday" sung. It's expected. No birthday would pass without this ritual.

Anyone who would not get the cake or the call would be deeply hurt, I'm sure. It would be a highly visible signal that we forgot.

With children and their spouses, and our grandchildren, there are 14 birthdays to remember and to celebrate. But we dare not forget one. It would be a family tragedy.

Thanksgiving is a big deal too. So is Mother's Day and Father's Day and wedding anniversaries. So are other special holidays. And of course Christmas is the biggest deal of all. I won't begin to tell you about our Christmas rituals.

But the point of all this celebrating is that we two parents have always put those things at the top of our priority list. Priorities put things first and other things second or last. Why are family traditions first? Because family is first. The traditions merely play out the family commitment. They merely stage the play. Family members are the lead characters, the stars of the show.

Our children have come to expect that we won't call the day before Christmas and say, "Sorry, not this year." They know that we will not neglect to call or have a cake for birthdays.

We have another major family tradition. Each October our entire family makes a pilgrimage to Turkey Run, Indiana. During this time of fall foliage, that slice of rural Americana stages a Covered Bridge Festival with their own traditions. A big tent goes up on the courthouse lawn and local people dress up in nineteenth-century costumes and sell jams, jellies, bittersweet, pumpkins, books, and crafts to a tradition-hungry public. But more than the festival, our family likes to hike the trails in Turkey Run State Park. We like to get together in the evenings and play games, laugh, eat, and simply have fun.

Who has time for this kind of thing today? We do. We are committed to it as long as we have the strength to crawl into the car and go. Nothing keeps us from that tradition. We have to reserve our rooms two years ahead so that the dates are fixed. Nobody in the family would think of putting something else ahead of Turkey Run. Why? Because that would be a signal that family had slid down the pole of priorities.

It's not that the tradition itself is at the top of the priority list; it's just that by keeping the tradition there we keep the family there. It's one way to say to the family, "You're number one this weekend. Nothing, absolutely nothing (except God, of course), will become number one in your place."

We don't verbally repeat that to each other in so many words. But that's the message, loud and clear, and we all know it.

When I understood that message, I realized more clearly what God was saying in the Second Commandment: "You shall have no other gods before me" (Exodus 20:3). God was asking us to get our priorities straight, and that's what we are asking each other as a family. Priorities speak louder than words. The high priorities of family traditions should say to each family member, "You're number one!" Parents, talk with your children by putting them number one in family traditions.

2) Family traditions speak of personal presence.

You perhaps noticed something about our family traditions: Each has a deep commitment to personal presence. We will be there with you. If we can't, we will call and personally talk with you.

Absentee parenting is the great vacuum in today's families. Children don't need an extra TV, or a fancier bike, or a video recorder with more buttons. They need YOU!

Perhaps you are a single parent and you can't be with them as much as you want. But you can be with them some of the time and when you are, truly give them your personal presence.

Perhaps you have a job that forces you to travel more than you want to. Sometimes that can't be helped, and sometimes it can. But when you are home, make the most of your personal presence.

Personal presence in traditions is the highest award bestowed on your children. No TV in the world can compete with you being there with them (unless you let them build the unfortunate habit of substituting the tube for you).

When you develop family traditions for growing children, and I hope you will, be sure to have traditions that are intensive with your presence. The principal reason we want to go to heaven is to be with God. The principal reason kids should want to come home is to be with you.

What does your presence say? It says, "You are so important that I want to be with you." What does your habitual absence from your children say to them? It says, "You are so unimportant that I want to be with strangers instead." Parents, talk with your children through your personal presence in family traditions.

3) Family traditions speak of personal security.

I remember the many little evidences of personal security as our children grew up—a favorite blanket, a favorite toy, a favorite activity. When thunderstorms came across our Illinois landscape in the middle of the night, the favorite activity (no, the only activity) for our very young children was to jump into bed with us.

Thunder could crash and lightning could flash, but all was well as long as they were cuddled up between Mom and Dad.

A well-loved family tradition is like a favorite blanket or being cuddled up between parents during a thunderstorm: It brings personal security.

Our children have known for many years that next year there *will* be a cake on birthdays, there *will* be a Turkey Run weekend, there *will* be a Christmas tree with traditional ornaments, there *will* be a big Thanksgiving dinner with turkey and stuffing. They never thought, "There will be one of these, *if* . . ." There was no "if." There *will* be the tradition with the same celebration in the same place at the same time in the same way. You can count on it! That's security. When we know for sure during our growing-up years that there are certain unmovable boundaries, certain hidebound traditions, certain things that will not change, certain things we can count on—when we are assured of these things, we are assured. We are secure.

Insecurity grows in the yeast of change. Life without roots, life in flux, life on the go all the time, life with no fixed boundaries, life with no honored traditions, is the breeding ground for insecurity.

Parents, talk with your children about personal security through family traditions. What you say through those traditions is "You *can* feel secure because some things will not change; some things will not squish out of your grasp when you reach out for them."

4) Family traditions speak of covenant.

I never fully understood covenant as expressed in the Bible until I understood the power of our family traditions. God's covenant with His people, and theirs with Him, were binding agreements. They were more than merely saying "I'll do it"; They were vows affirming that something would actually be done. Personal reputation was on the line. Integrity was on the line. Commitment was on the line.

Turkey Run weekend is something of a binding agreement with us, a covenant. We don't merely say, "I hope to be there." We *vow* to be there. We commit ourselves to be there. The integrity of our promise is at stake.

Arlie and I have some legal documents that are called covenants and agreements. They relate to real estate, or contracts, or other binding legal arrangements. When I agreed to write this book, the publisher and I entered into a binding covenant, a legal agreement that we would each do our part. We signed our names and thereby promised that we would actually do it, not that we merely hope to do it. I didn't say, "I hope to write it," and the publisher didn't say, "I hope to publish it." We each say, "We *will* do it. And we will sign our names, laying our personal integrity on the line to fulfill our promises."

Those are strong words to children. But if we can say such things to publishers and authors and real estate buyers or sellers and lawyers and dozens of other non-family-members, why can't we make such covenants and agreements to our own family members?

Parents, talk with your children by agreeing that you will carry on certain traditions, that you will be there at certain important times, that you will not put other things ahead of them.

5) Family traditions speak of bonding.

Last October our family was enjoying our annual Turkey Run outing. We were all there—16 of us! As usual, we spent most of our time hiking on the woodland trails of Turkey Run State Park. One morning Ron and I were walking together and I was carrying his little Katy, nuzzled next to my cheek, as I sang softly to her. Katy was only seven months old, but she knew that something special was happening and she kept her little cheek close to mine, listening to my song. Ron watched as this went on for some ten minutes or more, with Katy keeping close to my cheek.

"A good time for bonding," Ron said at last. We both knew that was right because this had been going on for many years in our family.

Our tradition of going to Turkey Run each year and hiking trails together is much more than recreation. It is bonding. It's a time to bind family members close to each other. Time together is bonding time when we are binding ourselves to one another through mutually pleasant experiences.

Bonding time is not a one-time experience. It is a *repetition* of experiences that we enjoy together. Bonding among people is like bonding with glue: It brings us close together and will not let us easily be taken apart. If you have not yet read the book *Bonding*, by Donald M. Joy, I wish you would. Bonding is a vital dimension of parent-child relationships, and much of it is accomplished through talk and through traditions that speak to us.

I think families that have strong traditions and continue them are unlikely to have divorce, runaways, parent-child conflict, and other serious breaches in the family. Let me know if I'm wrong, but I don't see how it is possible.

Bonding and divorce are antonyms. Bonding and runaways are antonyms. Bonding and drug use are antonyms.

It may sound boring, but traditions, or family rituals, replay the same scene or the same act over and over again—same thing, same place, same activities, same food. Why does such a repetitious habit bond us together? Perhaps because it's one of the few things in life that provides security. We can count on each other being there. We can count on each other replaying this record over and over again. It says I care. It says I will be with you. It says I won't put other things ahead of you.

That's bonding. And bonding prevents family ruptures. Traditions speak loud and clear, not with words as much as repetition, replaying the old favorite again and again and finding great security in doing it.

6) Family traditions speak of heritage.

This one is difficult to explain, but I know it works. Our third generation, our grandchildren, are hopelessly "hooked" on our traditions. They look forward to them, talk about them, would not let us stop them.

Our Turkey Run weekend has been going on now for many years. It's not the exact place that's important (although now we can't change it—part of the tradition, you know). It could have been any good place where memories can be built. It's not what we do there (although now we can't change those things either—that's part of the tradition).

I know what would happen if Arlie and I said we would not go next year: They wouldn't let us opt out.

If you have not started a family tradition, please don't put it off another year. Choose a place your family could enjoy together. Choose some things to do there that you would like to repeat each year. Then go back every year and do the same things over and over again. I know it sounds corny, but I also know that it works!

Turkey Run is part of our budget. Sometimes we have had to do without other things to take the family there. But we call it our investment. During most of our children's growing-up years we invested there instead of in a retirement program or investment program. But I'm convinced this was a better investment.

Each of us as parents and grandparents must decide the most important things we will bequeath to our children and grandchildren. Our children know they will inherit much less when we die because we have used our money for family activities while we are alive. We have invested heavily in family education and travel, activities and traditions. We have traveled hundreds of thousands of miles together as a family. We have invested in things that the family can do together, year after year. Our legacy will not be large sums of money, and we all understand that. But I think our children will see their heritage as family togetherness and strength of family ties, and will appreciate it more than money.

My plea is that you evaluate your portfolio now and ask what part family traditions, family travel, and family togetherness are of your investments. Ask what you want to leave behind for your family, what they will value most.

Traditions do speak loud and clear. They eloquently testify that families that participate in them generously will be bonded together and will not likely come apart.

In summary, then, here are some ways that family traditions speak to your children (and grandchildren!):

1) Family traditions tell your children that they are tops on your priority list, that you will not put things of lesser importance above them.

2) Family traditions tell your children that you *will* be with them when they need you.

3) Family traditions tell your children that they may feel secure in the assurance that things they consider important will not change.

4) Family traditions tell your children that you consider certain things as binding agreements with them, covenants, and that they can be assured you will keep your word by keeping the agreements.

5) Family traditions tell your children that you are bound to them and they to you, that they can be assured that the family will not come unglued, that there will be another tradition together, and another, and still another.

6) Family traditions tell your children that your legacy to them will be things more valuable than money. They will inherit strong family values and experiences, and those are things that money cannot buy.

15

*The Wonder of Words—
Little Buckets that
Carry Power*

Words are like little buckets; they carry something important from me to you.

Some of these little buckets carry names. Others carry actions—something happening. Still others carry descriptions—paintings to hang on the walls of our minds. Some are like hooks that join two things together.

Most important, these little buckets carry ideas and emotions. Through words, the little buckets of language, we transmit these ideas and feelings between us.

Let's take the simple phrase "I love you" as an example. The bucket filled with "I" names me as the person doing something. What am I doing? Another bucket carries that. I'm sending my love in the love bucket. Where am I sending it? To you. That's the third bucket. With these three little buckets I send an important message to you, either with my mouth or by writing it with my hands. You receive the little buckets in the eargate and pour out my message into your brain.

We have ingenious ways to send buckets back and forth, printed materials like books and magazines and letters, as well as technological wonders like telephones, television sets, and computer modems. But we don't want to get sidetracked on those things.

Some buckets are smaller than others and some are larger than others. But don't let the size of the bucket deceive you. Some big buckets are almost empty, carrying impoverished ideas. Other small buckets are brimming over with meaning.

Some of us who read theology books encounter some really big buckets, like ontological, modalistic, postmillennialism, or anthropological. The buckets are big but the stuff in them is not nearly as big as that little bucket brimming over with the word "love." Not one of these theological words is more significant or more powerful than that little four-letter word.

"Anthropological" is a mouthful and a mindful, but "love" is a heartful. "Love" is a more powerful word, a more life-changing word than "anthropological," which is a bigger word. Bigness is not power in the world of words. *Power is in the idea and how that idea strikes fire in you the listener*—not in the size of the bucket that carries the idea. Words were never intended as power in themselves; they are buckets only. Some of my friends forget this and try to impress their readers, or listeners, with the size of the bucket rather than the power of the idea.

Words are always sent between two people—never more. For example, when the president or prime minister speaks on television, he sends out his little buckets. Millions of people listen. He may speak to a composite person made up of a million individuals, but we always listen as a million individuals. Thus we always communicate one on one, even in a crowd. We never talk to more than one person, even though we may be talking to a crowd of a thousand "one persons." So our little word buckets always go between two people.

Sometimes those little word buckets confuse us. Imagine, for example, a couple recently married. One says to the other, "Who do you love most?" The other replies, "You." The little bucket full of "you" is carried with the utmost tenderness and feeling.

The years pass and the couple has an argument. One snarls at the other, "You!" The bucket is the same. Mechanically everything is the same. But what a difference in the message! In the first, the little bucket is like a gentle caress of fingertips over the soft, receptive mind. In the second, the little bucket is filled with sand, grinding into the heart. Somehow the manner in which the little bucket is sent transcends the bucket itself. The word is lost in the way it is transmitted.

Many communications problems between husbands and wives, or parents and children, arise because of this matter of transmission. The words, the mechanics, were correct, but the *feeling* was damaging. Sometimes damaging feeling is intended, so communication is complete although unfortunate. At other times the intended feeling is misread. The communication is not complete. There is a short-circuit.

The simple word "you" can be said with tenderness, fierce anger, disgust, inquisitiveness, or as a statement of fact. What you intend to communicate is the emotion you send with the bucket, not merely the bucket itself. You also communicate intention through body language, eye contact, and inflection of voice.

Of all forms of communication God could have chosen, He selected words to share His truth and His love. The Bible is The Word, filled with words, to share His message with His people. It is obvious from this fact that God has a special place for words in His grand plan of redemption.

Not only that, but in His creative genius, God made a tongue in each of His people, a strange little device used to articulate blessings or curses. As James said, "With the tongue we praise our Lord and Father, and with it we curse men. . . . Out of the same mouth come praise and cursing" (James 3:9,10).

Words are handmaidens of the mind and heart. The words we speak are merely expressions of what we are and think. As Jesus said, "The things that come out of the mouth come from the heart" (Matthew 15:18).

As we seek to help our children learn to speak the right words, we must focus first on helping them think the right thoughts, and this in turn comes from helping them have the right relationships—with us and with God. As Christians, our words come from our thoughts, and our thoughts come from our relationships.

As a Christian father, one of my primary responsibilities has been to role-model the use of words that will please God. If they please God, they will certainly please me also. In addition, it is my responsibility to encourage my children to think of good words and godly words as small but valuable treasures. We prize them and seek to use them graciously.

Words are not always what they appear to be. There are times when the words we speak with obvious humor may have the opposite meaning. You've heard people say things like "You're a nut," "What a bore!" or "You dummy!" Spoken in seriousness, these are insulting statements. But many times you and I have heard these and dozens of similar statements spoken in humor to create the opposite meaning, or even as terms of endearment. Ethnic groups may use terms within the group which would be considered insulting if thrown at them from the outside. Family groups do the same. Within the clan (family, ethnic group, neighborhood, circle of friends) people often toss barbs at each other in jest. But they will not tolerate the same statements from outsiders.

I usually don't like this type of communication within the family, even in jest. Sometimes there is a thin line between jest and a semihumorous veiled dig at one another.

I've seen husbands and wives, in the presence of their children, dig at each other with semihumorous barbs and I have wondered what the children were thinking. If the father and mother do it with each other, surely it must seem right to the children to do also.

I would urge caution in parents using barbed humor with their children or with each other in the presence of their children. It is easy for a child to misunderstand and take the message the wrong way.

Some good rules of thumb in the words you use with children are: 1) How serious is the intent of the message you really want to communicate even though you may be laughing and projecting a sense of humor? 2) Is there at least a strong possibility that your child may misunderstand, and take what you are saying in the wrong way? 3) Don't communicate to your child in a way you don't want your child to communicate to you or his friends. 4) Don't say it if you wouldn't want to hear it (practice the Golden Rule). 5) Don't talk to your mate or ex-mate through your child (tell your father I don't want to talk now!). You may turn your child into an unthinking machine and turn the other parent against the child unfairly.

What are some good words you would like your child to use often? Use them often yourself. Find pleasant contexts for new words that help your child communicate good things. For example, "please" and "thank you" are words that all children should learn early. Do you use them often? Do you make a habit of using "please" when you ask your child to do something, and "thank you" when he has finished the work? Role-modeling is more powerful than nagging.

In our family the phrase "love you" is often a close to a phone conversation or a goodbye affirmation. We use it frequently and meaningfully. We have for many years. It's not surprising to hear our grown children use it often the way we have.

Some words are borderline, minced oaths, a genteel way of making a point without swearing. We're all guilty of some of these minced oaths. "Darn" and "dang" aren't really swearing, but you might think twice before making a habit of saying words like these before your child. A good rule of thumb: Don't use words before your child that you wouldn't want your child to "play back" in Sunday school class or in the presence of your family at the next family dinner.

Word games are fun to do with your children. There are dozens of word-game booklets that will help your child have fun by learning words of daily living. We've had fun with words while we travel. Travel hours can be lost hours or hours of family tension. Or they can be delightful times together with much learned. This is a great time to help children learn to use the kinds of words you think are best.

In summary, here are some important guidelines to remember as you help your child learn how to use words to please God and you.

1) Through words we communicate ideas and feelings, so it is important to help our children learn to use words that will please God and us.

2) The same word can transmit the opposite meaning, depending on the way we say it and the body language we use while saying it.

3) God has chosen The Word and words to communicate His truth. That makes words precious to us, something to be treasured.

4) Words can transmit the opposite meaning when said in jest. But there is a risk of miscommunicating to our children if we are not careful.

5) The Golden Rule is a good rule to follow in the words we use with our children. So is The Playback Rule (don't say what you don't want played back at the wrong time!).

6) Word games are fun ways to redeem lost hours of travel, helping your child learn to use these important little devices that carry life's meaning.

16

Walking Is Talking

When I was a boy, growing up on an Illinois grain farm, rabbit-hunting was the thing to do, partly because of the sport and partly because a rabbit was a tasty treat on a farm dinner table. Hunting cottontails was a winter sport, and in the absence of a hunting dog I followed the rabbit's tracks in the fresh snow until I came to his hiding place.

Grown men in that part of the country did this too. Most farmers in postdepression America could not afford a hunting dog, so they had to depend on their own tracking instincts. So they and I followed those little pawprints in the snow. Wherever the rabbit went, we went. If the tracks went left, we went left. If the tracks went right, we went right.

Looking back, there's a note of nostalgic humor here. Think of it! Hundreds, no thousands, of intelligent men and boys following in the footsteps of rabbits! To paraphrase a Bible verse, "A little rabbit shall lead them."

But there is also something symbolic here. We are followers by instincts. I have heard that the early roads in New England followed old Indian trails, or even cowpaths. There is something in us that says "Follow the leader."

You have played the childhood game "Follow the Leader," haven't you? Wherever the leader goes, you go. If the leader walks through a puddle of water or mud, so do you. But Follow the Leader is more than a childhood game. As I write this book, I have been following the American presidential races. There is a national herd instinct emerging. As one candidate gathers more followers, others flock around him in increasing numbers. The scheme of a campaign is to pyramid followers.

Every person wants to hitch his wagon to a star. It's the stuff from which royalty is established and perpetuated. It's also the stuff that puts movie stars, sports heroes, and even highly visible Christian leaders on pedestals, often precariously high pedestals.

From our earliest years of childhood we look for someone to emulate, someone to follow, someone to be our hero, someone to be our role model. I read a research study not long ago about this. Most of all, it said, children want their parents to be their models. They want to look up to them and follow them.

We parents should not be misled by the child's tendency toward individualism, to become himself. That is also a natural inclination. But this is a healthy tension in growing up—on the one hand to become more and more one's own unique self while we look more and more to a parent (or both) to be a model which that unique self can emulate. Without saying it, almost every child is living out the statement "I want to be uniquely me, but I want to follow you in shaping my uniqueness."

Wise parents give their children the freedom to become themselves while they provide the role model for children to follow in becoming themselves. The task is to be what we hope our children will become, but to avoid forcing the child to become our clone. They will be like us, but only if we model the goal rather than force it.

There is a myth that says "Eloquence is a wise word fitly spoken." In parent-child relationships, eloquence is the voice of consistent living—consistent within the parent's own life and consistent before the child.

I have pondered why consistent Christian living produces much more fruit in a child's life than consistent "preaching at" the child. Why is my role-modeling so much more productive than all the words I speak to my children?

There is an old saying, "Don't do as I do, do as I say." Sometimes we parents say it to our children in jest. Of course our children may retort, "What you do speaks so loud that I can't hear what you say," another old saying.

After my 35 years of parenting, I believe that my most eloquent statements were not words, but wordless expressions of lifestyle before my children. But why?

What I say is only a statement of an "ought to" or "should do" proposition. "You should tell the truth," for example. But if my children recognize that my view of truth is a bit slippery and I don't hesitate to fudge a bit on commonly accepted boundaries of truthfulness, my proposition is hollow. It has no forcefulness of life to back up the words. It has nothing visual, nothing tangible, to reinforce the verbal. Words by themselves are empty buckets. In order to be full, they must carry life in them.

God made a statement of love in John 3:16: "God so loved the world that he gave his one and only Son, that whoever believes in him shall not perish but have eternal life." But this was not merely a statement; God backed it up with the life of His Son. The verbal message was backed up with a visual, tangible message on the cross. What God said was reinforced by what God did. His written and spoken Word would be lost on deaf ears without the personal costliness of His statement of love.

I think that is the role model for us as parents. Our Lord is the role model's Role Model. We look to Him to role model our role-modeling. That's why we must sink our roots in Him.

The written and spoken Word is an expression of who and what God is, not merely what He tells us to be. God *is* love before He commands us to love. God *is* truth before He commands us to be truthful. The entire Scripture is a description of who God is as an expression of what God wants us to become.

It's easy to issue rules, commands, requests, statements, or propositions. It's easy to say, "Do this or do that." But the rubber hits the road when we determine that we will ask nothing of our children that we are not first living out in our own lives. The Lord Himself exemplifies that. He asks nothing in His Word that is out of harmony with His own Person. He already *is* all that He asks us to *become*. That's why He is our ultimate Role Model.

There is much discussion these days about integrity. I think integrity is consistency, that remarkable quality that holds each of us together as a whole person, keeps us from coming unglued, keeps us from coming apart at the seams. Happiness is interwoven with this consistency. To the degree that we personally hold together, we are happy. Unhappiness is the recognition that we are coming apart, coming unglued, breaking into pieces, disintegrating, rupturing our wholeness.

Integrity moves on three fronts: 1) consistency with a standard we have adopted; 2) consistency within our own personhood; and 3) consistency of conduct projected to others, especially to our spouses and children, who know if we are really consistent or merely putting on a front.

As Christians we accept the Living Word (Christ) and the Written Word (the Scriptures) as our standard for faith and practice. We shape our worldview by these standards. We hammer new ideas on the anvil of scriptural truth. We measure new ideas on the yardstick of the Scriptures. We weigh our next steps by the truths we gather from our Lord and His Holy Word.

When we walk as a Christian on the Main Streets of daily life, we "clothe ourselves" with Christ (Romans 13:14). When we consistently live by the standards of the Living Word and the Written Word, we preserve our integrity and we are therefore happy. Our consistency to the standard we have adopted holds us together and keeps us from becoming fragmented persons.

As Christians we must also be consistent with ourselves—our worldview, our philosophy of life, our theological underpinnings, our personal formation, our system of values, all that we accept to make us the person we are. When we violate ourselves, we lose our integrity and invite unhappiness to rule over our divided self.

Within my person are many facets of my undivided wholeness. For example, I am what I believe. My beliefs are the sum total of those elements mentioned above—philosophy of life, theology, system of values, convictions. I have built the wholeness of my personal "house" with these materials. When I allow the storms of doubt to blow away some of these essentials, or the poison of hatred to eat away at them, or the fires of passion to consume them, I allow myself to come apart at the seams and I lose my integrity and my happiness.

Not only that, but I must maintain consistency among my beliefs, my communications, and my conduct. If I believe in God's provision but harbor doubts that He will provide, I divide myself and lose my integrity and my happiness with it. If I testify with my lips that I will serve God first and foremost but let my conduct drift into the worship of the gods of materialism, I divide myself and lose my integrity and happiness.

When my mind and heart are out of sync with my lips or hands, my integrity is compromised and my happiness is corrupted. When what I say and what I do ride off in opposite directions, my integrity is damaged and my happiness with it. When I do what my convictions say is wrong, or refuse to speak out for my beliefs, or allow my conversation to run across the grain of my convictions, I lose my integrity and my happiness with it.

We gag on a Christian's conduct that is antithetical to the Living Word or Written Word. We are nauseated by a Christian's conversation that is out of sync with Christian convictions. If we believe it, we should say it and live it. If we know this to be true, think what those around us expect us to model for them. Think what our children expect from us.

Thus the yardstick of our parental role modeling is 1) consistency to the ultimate standard for our life, which for Christians is the Living Word and the Written Word; 2) consistency within ourselves—to the wholeness of our personhood and the integrity of our theology, philosophy of life, convictions, beliefs, and system of values; and 3) consistency before our children in integrating what we believe, what we say, and what we do.

What you say is what you are put into words, just as what God says in His Written Word is what He *is* as the Living Word. God verbalizes Himself in His Word, presenting the integrity of His Person through the vehicle of words.

When we as parents get out of sync as Christians and come apart at the seams, we lose our personal integrity and become a statement to our children that we don't believe our beliefs enough to say them or believe our words enough to do them.

Children are amazingly perceptive; they detect parental inconsistency, breaches of integrity, and unhappiness immediately. When this happens, you don't need to tell them you are unhappy; they know it almost before you do. They also know when you tell them to be what you are not, or what to say that you don't say, or what to believe that is not evidenced by your own convictions.

We make the most powerful, life-changing statements to our children, not with words as much as with the consistency of our daily living before them—consistency of our lives with our ultimate standards; consistency within our wholeness as a person; and consistency of our convictions, conversation, and conduct. This consistency within us weaves the fabric of integrity from which the garments of happiness are tailored.

Children have within themselves a desire to find and follow heroes and heroines. They are not built with an innate desire to emulate scoundrels. They learn that kind of thing most when parents drift from the heroic and carry with them their child's ideals.

The heroic to a child is not necessarily high adventure. Many parents think they must compete with movie and TV heroes to be a hero to their child, but that is not true at all. The cowboy in last night's Western movie can shoot a bottle from a fence better than you can, but he won't cuddle up with your son and read a book to him tonight. That glittering star on last week's TV program may captivate your daughter's mind with her beauty and costumes, but she won't be there when your daughter cuts her finger or is teased by her friends and needs a mom or dad to comfort her.

I think a child's view of the heroic is a measure of how much someone is "like Dad" or "like Mom." From what I have perceived and what I have read, the standard for heroes and heroines is a mom or dad living consistently before a child. It's fun to see the cowboy shoot the bottle from the fence, but the heroic is in the triumph of good over evil, not in shooting the bottle. The heroic cowboy is heroic because he makes things come out right, the way Dad and Mom do. He rescued the damsel in distress or drove out the rustlers from the local ranches, and that is high adventure. Dads and moms don't usually have this kind of high adventure with their children, but that doesn't matter. They still make right win over wrong, and that makes them heroic.

Is it possible that we have confused this issue? We think we have to be like the cowboy or movie star to be a role model for our child, but it's really the opposite: The cowboy and movie star must be like us to be heroic. We don't have to shoot bottles from fences or wear glittering evening gowns. We have to be Mom and Dad, consistent before our child, there when he needs us, always *for* her, anxious to be *with* him, delighted to talk with her.

Role-modeling is not expecting the child to become a clone—either of us or of his brother or sister. We do not help our child grow when we try to squeeze him into a box shaped like another person. As I mentioned earlier, we need to help the child grow with all his individuality, to become his best under God, while he models the best in you.

Role-modeling need not be a frightening responsibility. It's as simple as being what we know God wants us to be, which is what our child wants us to be, which ultimately should be what *we* want us to be. As we strive to follow our Ultimate Role Model we become the actual role model our child needs.

For the small child, most theology is not learned by having it verbalized as much as by having parents live it out before him. I cannot tell my child that God will always listen to him if I'm preoccupied and will not listen. I cannot tell my child that God loves him if I am unloving and abrasive. I cannot tell my child that God cares if I don't. I must not say that God is always there if I'm never available.

Walking is talking. Without saying a word you speak volumes. Without uttering one sentence you present profound truths.

Your child is not asking you to become the smartest, most handsome, most beautiful, most talented, or any other "most" in the world. What he wants is for you to be consistently *you*, to consistently live according to the Ultimate Role Model, thereby providing the role-modeling that accents true heroism.

In summary, here are some guidelines concerning role modeling, or talking through walking:

1) Within each of us there is an instinct to follow, to search for a role model, to hitch our wagon to a star.

2) A child seeks to build individuality at the same time he seeks to attach himself to a role model. In a

sense he searches for a role model as a model in shaping his individuality.

3) The most eloquent voice is that of consistent daily living. This consistency is seen as we live a) in harmony with a standard we have adopted, such as Christ and the Scriptures; b) in harmony within ourselves; and c) in a harmony that brings what we think, say, and do in sync.

4) Children search for the heroic, and to the growing child the qualities exhibited by parents are the models of the heroic (whether those qualities are good or bad).

5) A small child learns theology best by parental conduct. The small child searches for God's qualities in his parents.

17

Talking Through Tensions

The stewardesses had just finished pouring our breakfast coffee when we hit sudden turbulence. I suppose modern detection devices would have warned us, but this was more than 20 years ago, and our jet-prop plane did not have many of today's sophisticated instruments. Without warning we hit an air pocket and dropped. It was as though someone had pulled the carpet of air from under us. My coffee left the cup, ascended to the ceiling, then came down with a magnificent splat on the seat beside me. (Fortunately, the seat was empty!) At this point breakfast was over; I don't think anyone had the stomach to eat or drink when we finally regained stable flight.

I always stand in awe of flight, especially with enormous jumbo jets. Everyone knows that a machine this heavy can't float in the air. So how does it stay up?

Some bright fellow in another era figured out that we can fly if we learn to master tension. It's really simple. As a boy I followed the same principle with paper airplanes, the same type I now make for my grandsons. To oversimplify, wing pushes against air, which in turn pushes against wing. Wing against air,

air against wing. With the right devices to guide the plane, this tension forces the plane upward. This balanced tension of wing and air keeps even an enormous metal machine aloft.

Jet engines have thrust. That's another way of saying the plane is propelled forward with an engine that pushes a powerful burst of hot air against the air behind it. Air pushes against air. Something has to give, so the engine, with the plane attached, is pushed forward. So forward movement is produced by powerful hot winds generated by the plane's engines, creating a point of tension with the air behind. I can fly around the world because someone recognized the value of tension—wing against air, powerful thrust of air against air. That's what keeps us up and keeps us going. No tension, no flight.

Birds that fly to my backyard feeders are made something like our planes, or should I say our planes are made like the birds. The cardinal that ate sunflower seeds outside my window yesterday streaked through the woods like a miniature Boeing 737. He lacked jet engines and instruments, but God endowed him with all the instruments of flight he needed. He stayed aloft because of the tension of wings and tail against the air. No tension, no flight.

As I ponder useful tension, I am amazed at how much of life depends upon it. But before we get too excited about the values of useful tension, let's recognize that uncontrolled tension can also destroy us. We seek controlled tension and shun uncontrolled tension. Life daily hangs in the balance between useful tension, or tension under control, and uncontrolled tension. Growth and happiness come from discovering and exercising that balance.

Psychologists speak of tension as an emotional state similar to anxiety. This is produced by a muscular tightness, a mental strain, like a rubber band stretched to the breaking point. This is tension out of control. Until we hit the air pocket, my plane had tension under control. The cardinal at my bird feeder always seems to have the tension of flight under control.

My psychologist friends want their patients to reduce their uncontrolled tensions, thereby becoming more relaxed. Psychologists are paid to relieve excessive or prolonged undesirable tension. They want patients to bring tension under control.

I would never pay anyone to remove all tension from my life. Neither should you. We would become blobs without controlled tensions—even certain controlled tensions with mate or children.

If the airplane wing did not produce a tension against the air, the plane would fall. So would the beautiful cardinal in my backyard. If the jet engine did not produce a tension against the air behind it, the plane would not make forward progress, and without that it would fall.

All human relationships involve certain tensions. We must never wish them all away. Instead, we must seek to bring them under control, to redeem our tensions for our mutual benefit.

I have pondered why we often choose a husband or wife with opposite or quite dissimilar natures, rather than someone just like us. Is there built into us a subconscious recognition that we need certain tensions to keep life balanced, and we therefore seek mates who will provide those tensions?

And does this mean that a marriage devoid of all tensions (I'm not talking about petty and pointless quarrels, but wing-against-air, air-against-air type of tensions that produces flight in marriage) would fail? I'm asking. I really want to know.

Parental correction is a point of tension between parent and child. But without it a child becomes a spoiled brat. Every time you say "no" to your child you establish that point of tension. It's only a little two-letter word, but it creates a point of resistance. The word "don't" serves the same function. "Stop" may do it too. The parent erects a wall against which the child pushes in his quest for individuality or independence.

So discipline or correction is tension. But the lack of it is corruption, for it stifles growth or sends the growing child down the wrong path.

My musician friends tell me that the term "counterpoint" involves musical tensions. Counterpoint is, I understand, note against note, melody against melody, setting up tensions of a sort. On the one hand, these musical tensions are set up against one another to establish a melodic independence, and on the other hand to establish harmonic mutual dependence. Forces provide points of tension to enhance independence while at the same time they unite for mutual benefit. So a conversation emerges in this relationship, a dialogue of sorts, each element retaining its independence while it harmonizes to establish its mutual dependence.

When that was explained to me, I thought of family life—marital relationships and parent-child relationships. Do you see the remarkable parallel? Like the musical masterpiece, husband and wife join in this tension, on the one hand seeking the independence of individuality while on the other hand establishing a mutual dependence. Opposites unite to enhance each individual as both strive for mutual benefit. But in the dialogue between these opposites, each partner retains the melody of unique individuality while harmonizing to maximize mutual dependence.

And what about parent-child relationships? From birth, the child creates a tension in search of independence and individuality, while at the same time he learns that the concept of family is the harmony produced through mutual dependence. This creates within the parent a tension also, for the parent is committed to help the child build independence, but is equally committed to cultivate within the child a desire for that mutual dependence in family life.

In balancing this tension of individuality and family team development another tension arises, both in the parent and in the child. Intellectually the parent wants to help the child become independent, a true individual, for that is what parenting is all about. But emotionally there is an equally strong desire to slow this weaning down, to savor childhood before we lose it. How many parents say, almost daily, "You're growing up too fast"? That's another way of saying, "I want you to grow normally, but I wish somehow I could keep you the way you are now."

The child may not recognize this second tension as much as the parent does, but it also operates in the child as much as in the parent. On the one hand the child anxiously presses to grow older, sometimes the "six-going-on-sixteen" syndrome. But while he presses to grow older and leave childhood, he also wants to cling to the delights and benefits of childhood. If you don't think this is true, notice how many teddy bears or favorite childhood stuffed animals appear in college dorms!

Something beautiful happens in balancing all of these tensions. In the dialogue between these opposing forces, parent and child establish and build a happy balance between the melody of individuality and independence, as each strives to build the harmony of the family. Both work out a balance between the melody of unique personal growth and the harmony of mutual dependence, which is the essence of family living. These are the healthy tensions that promote growth. Without them, parenting would be insipid and children would grow to be robots.

As we play the music of marriage before our families and friends (and for each other!) we unite our uniquely different and sometimes opposing ideas, talents, contributions, and personalities. As we do, the melody of the individual emerges along with the harmony of the team, presenting something beautiful and exemplary. This musical dialogue, a conversation of sorts, between the melody of individuality and the harmony of the team, enhances each person without depriving either. The more we strive to build each other as unique persons, the more we build our family team. The more we build our family team, the more we find opportunity to build each other as unique individuals.

The music of parent-child relationships is much the same. In our daily dialogue, or talk, we help the child push for new frontiers of independence and unique individuality while he recognizes his increasing harmonious relationship to the family as a whole. Individuality loses nothing in striving to be a contributing part of the team, but is enhanced and strengthened through the process.

Husbands or wives, or parents and children, who strive for the melody of individuality at the expense of the harmony of mutual dependence in the family team lose both. Contrary to popular opinion, we do not become our best selves by ignoring others, especially those significant others who are vital to our daily walk. Individuality withers into atrophy without mutual dependence on significant others. The more we press for self without regard for the significant others in our lives the more we lose our own legitimate sense of self because we lose our balance between melody and harmony in life. Without that balance the symphony goes sour. Self-image goes to pot. Family togetherness disintegrates.

It is in the daily dialogue (talk) between husband and wife, or parent and child, that the melody of individuality and the harmony of family mutual dependence blend into a masterpiece of song for a wondering world to sing with you.

As husbands and wives sing this song that blends their melody of individuality with the harmony of mutual dependence, they establish a role model for their children, first for their relationship with parents and second for their future relationship in marriage.

My son Ron and I have written several books together. We spend hundreds of hours talking together each year about products with which we are both involved. Ron learned years ago not to be a "yes" man. He brings his individuality to the mix. He brings his different points of view. So do I. I don't think we have ever had an argument, but we hammer on each other's ideas to refine them. We challenge each other's thinking, and many things drop off by the time we are finished. We ask each other hard questions, tell each other why we think something isn't right, defend a point of view, add new perspectives, and keep working over what each other brings until we both feel we have something much better than our original proposals.

Ron is an editor in a publishing company now, and he must carry on this type of dialogue with his peers and his bosses there. But he doesn't mind at all, because in the tensions brought by opposing forces, the challenges tossed at one another, something much better often emerges, something mutually beneficial.

In that sense the dialogue that Ron and I have culti-vated makes us mutually dependent on each other in the formation of a product, while at the same time we retain our unique independence. I recommend this type of relationship for all parents whether or not you are developing a creative package. But to do it, you must start early in the child's life and cultivate it through the years. It's a year-in, year-out, day-in, day-out relationship woven with the threads of parent-child talk.

This kind of dialogue is self-induced, mutually accepted tension. It is carried out with the goal always before you that the tension has been brought to the mix to hammer out something better. But there must also be a balance in the amount of tension brought to this relationship. Unrealistic goals, pushing beyond a child's capability, and demands that march too far ahead of delights upset the balance and become coun-terproductive.

These unbalanced, uncontrolled tensions inflame and heighten irritation between two people. They tend to cause a deterioration of relationship rather than a strengthening of relationship.

If you face unbalanced, uncontrolled tensions within the family, whether with spouse or child, ask yourself honestly what is precipitating them. Is there truly a mutual benefit, or does the lack of balance come because one person's "rights" are asserted without thinking of the team, the mutual dependence? Or does the lack of balance come from unrealistic expec-tations? Are we expecting more from one another than we should?

I know a man who wanted fences wide enough around his marriage so that he could live a rather high lifestyle while his wife stayed home to care for the children. He pushed for his own "freedom" from marital restraints for himself while he wanted his wife to feel a dependence on him for support. He created for himself the freedom to roam and choose his own lifestyle while he forged for his wife the chains of dependence on him while she lived in a prison of his own construction. It was a one-way street, and the marriage ended in divorce. The tensions created within the marriage stirred no music—only discord. It was his quest for what he thought was the enhancement of his individuality without any contribution to the team that destroyed the harmony of the team, and with it the melody of each individual.

When parents want to do their own thing so much that they minimize their involvement with their children, they send powerful signals that "my thing" (individuality and independence) is more important than "our thing." Should it surprise these parents when their child sends up the same signals? "My thing" becomes the child's goal too as he imitates the parent. The tension of the child's "my thing" striking against the parent's "my thing" is flint against steel. Each strives to play the melody of individuality without contributing to the harmony of the family team. Discord, not melody, is the result.

I realize that not all childhood rebellion comes from a parental search for "my thing." Children learn selfish individuality from peers, TV, reading the wrong stuff, and just plain human nature without restraint. It may come also from parents setting unrealistic goals for children or from constantly comparing one child with another (another form of setting unrealistic goals).

Taming tensions is best fulfilled through the dialogue of daily living begun at the very earliest age— parent and child talking together about anything and everything. The family that talks together plays the music of both melody and harmony together.

When our children were growing up, Arlie and I helped them learn to tie their shoes, dress themselves, cultivate good health habits, eat properly, and a thousand other things necessary for them to do without us. Our job was to help them gain their independence, not all at once but over a period of time.

On the one hand we worked feverishly to help them learn to be independent. On the other hand we worked just as feverishly to integrate these little individuals into the family team, to weld a strong sense of family togetherness. Our most effective method toward each goal was talk—the dialogue of daily living, the conversation of constructiveness, talk that tamed tensions.

But we discovered a little-recognized truth: This dialogue through the years has made it crystal clear to us that *parents need children as much as children need parents.* Never be deluded into thinking that dependence is a one-way street; the parent-child relationship is mutual dependence.

While our children needed Arlie and me, we also needed them. In one sense we were as dependent on them as they were on us. They needed us for the physical necessities of life, moral and spiritual guidance, counsel, role-modeling, talking with them about everyday needs—dozens of things like that. We needed them as participants in our parental task, participants in cultivating a spirit of service within the family, and we needed their tensions toward individuality to help us as a family mount up, wing against air, air against air, and fly.

We needed the growing individuality of our children to contribute much more to the family harmony than Arlie and I could ever contribute ourselves. Each child brings something unique to the family portrait. Without that uniqueness, the family portrait is not complete.

No, never think that because you are a parent you are the only one contributing to the family harmony. Children contribute also, through the dialogue of daily living with them, through the give-and-take of talking together, through the beautiful music that emerges from each unique individual within the family contributing to the family harmony. An orchestra needs more than the conductor. Each instrument, even the ones less visible, supports the beauty of the whole.

But what about unhealthy tensions within the family? You have them and you don't know what to do with them. I don't think you will ever resolve these tensions by trying to squelch them or suppress them, by criticizing your child because of them, by trying to come down like a hammer on them. Unhealthy tensions are often, if not usually, attempts to assert "my rights" without thought of "our opportunities."

Ask yourself if the unhealthy tensions have come from your own attempt as a parent to assert "my rights" without regard for the child's growing individuality. I have found it helpful in troubled times to search my own heart first before probing other people in the mix. Sometimes we don't need to look farther. Sometimes we do.

It also could be that your spouse or child is pressing for "my rights" to the neglect of the family team. Try to discover the purpose of that quest. Perhaps some of those rights are valid. Perhaps some are not. Perhaps the rights are valid but misguided.

Slamming the doors of our lives against such a quest is not the answer; *talking things through* is the answer. But your ability to talk things through depends on the talking relationship you have already established with your spouse or child. Taming tension is through talk. But talk is closely interwoven into relationships. With the right relationships that you have developed you can talk easily with your child. But it is through talk that you build these right relationships. They go together.

Like the chicken-and-egg syndrome, it's pointless to talk about which comes first. You need eggs to have chickens and chickens to have eggs. You need talk to build relationships and relationships to provide a climate for talk.

Start now to cultivate an open talking relationship with your child (or spouse). Do this before specific tensions arise. When unhealthy tensions arise, this is the wrong time to be developing long-range relationships. There's too much short-range heat to generate long-range light.

Begin now to cultivate times of talking with your children (and spouse). Do it during the sunshine of family relationships, so that when the storms come you're that much farther ahead. Begin talking, and begin to cultivate a relationship that embraces open conversation, the day your child is born. Build upon it each day. You'll never be sorry you did.

In summary, here are some helpful reminders concerning family tensions and how to make them constructive rather than destructive:

1) We should recognize that some tension is destructive and some is constructive. Without constructive tension, we are deprived of growth.

2) The individuality that we each bring to a marriage, or to a parent-child relationship, is an important element in family harmony. But this individuality is enhanced not by striving for "my rights" but by striving to make my uniqueness a valuable part of family harmony.

3) Like counterpoint in a musical masterpiece, our individuality plays the melody, but that melody is at

its best when it participates in a dialogue that results in harmony. Harmony is enhanced by the individuality of melody, but melody is enhanced by the mutual dependence necessary for harmony.

4) Discipline or correction should be done in a spirit of enhancing the individuality of the child by helping him participate in the family harmony.

5) Enhancing individuality by building family harmony should be role-modeled by the parent. The child understands the dialogue of conversation best when it is reinforced with the dialogue of daily living.

6) When we family members challenge each other's thinking, we should do it not to assert "my way" or to depreciate "your way," but to discover a new and better "our way."

7) Establish a good talking relationship during pleasant days, so that when the storms of unhealthy tensions arise you will have a basis for dialogue.

8) In dialogue (talk) that seeks to build family harmony, parents need the input of children as much as children need the input of parents. The harmony of family togetherness is enhanced by talk, child with parent as well as parent with child.

18

Discipline and Discipleship

Hanging beside our fireplace is a relic from the past, my father-in-law's razor strop. It's a wide, formidable piece of leather about three feet long. Most children today have never seen a razor strop, because this interesting device left the scene a step or two behind the buggy whip.

I remember my father sharpening his straight-edge razor on a strop just like the one hanging beside our fireplace, whisking it back and forth with lightning speed. But his strop disappeared many years ago, victim to modernization that hooked even the older men of his generation on electric razors.

These razor strops had a dual purpose: Leather-makers sold them to sharpen razors, but they were used almost as much to enforce discipline. Have you laughed, as our family has, at Bill Cosby's delightful presentation about his father's razor strop as a symbol of discipline? This was on a cassette, and we often listened to it as we traveled. Our children loved to hear him describe the strop in jest—nine feet long with hooks in it. It became a family joke with our grown children when we talked about the discipline of years gone by.

I suppose Arlie did not have this razor strop applied to her much or she would never permit it to hang by our fireplace. But she does confess that it found its mark at least once.

When people of our generation remember razor strops we remember discipline. And the word "discipline" brings to mind spankings or harsh words to enforce behavior, punishment for bad behavior. But that is a limited view of discipline, a very limited view. Your dictionary will help you see the much wider horizon for the word.

Discipline encompasses a wide range of training or guidance toward orderly conduct. Sometimes this involves punishment; most of the time it doesn't. True discipline in its fullest sense is not a harsh term, but should actually be a delightful experience. Discipline at its best can truly be a delight.

To be trained for my lifework I had to go to graduate school—several years of it. Completing graduate school and meeting the requirements was a discipline. But I also found it a delight. I really enjoyed it. I know that some people find it a boring chore, but I'm sorry they do, for they are missing something good, and may well be doing something out of sync with their gifts.

When Harvest House and I decided to do this book, we each embarked on a period of discipline. It isn't easy to write a book. It isn't easy to edit it, produce it, and market it. But together we have really had a delightful time bringing this material together as a book and presenting it to you. Our discipline has truly been a delight.

Today I bought some rosebushes for Arlie's birthday. That's what she wanted more than anything. I dug the ground, mixed peat moss into the soil, added compost and sand, made holes for the bushes, and ultimately planted them exactly the way the instructions said they should be planted. It was backbreaking, dirty, sweaty work that took several hours.

To give this gift to Arlie I had to undertake a rigorous discipline. It wasn't easy. You would not have wanted me in your house when I finished, for I was covered with dirt and sweat. The discipline of planting the roses made me a social outcast. Even my family would have rejected me at the dinner table.

But this dirty, sweaty discipline was a delight. Why? Because I kept thinking of the delights Arlie would get from the roses when they bloom. I was delighted with the discipline because I knew the fruits of the discipline would delight her.

The discipline of punishment has never been a delight for me. I shrink from it. Punishing my children has always hurt me more than it has them. I know that sounds trite, but it's true. Perhaps you have found this true also. I think that's because we taste the bitter fruits of punishment with our children. Nevertheless we must punish at times. God does! But it doesn't mean I like it.

If my child and I are to delight in his orderly life, we must each tolerate some punishment along the way. Ordered living is the fruit of discipline, and discipline at times is punishment. I must remember this when God disciplines me to bring order into my life.

As a father, the discipline I bring to my children is so much more than punishment. Guiding my child into more mature ways has always been a delight for me. I share the good fruit with my growing child.

The word "discipline" is a close relative of the word "disciple." Discipline is that which we do to make disciples. Jesus' disciples followed Him closely for many months. They listened to Him teach. They watched

Him feed the multitudes. They talked with Him along the way and learned about God and His home. By the time Jesus ascended into heaven, the disciplines of walking with the Son of God bore fruit. The disciplines had produced disciples, leaders who had learned the fruitfulness of leadership by first learning the discipline of following.

Jesus' parting mandate to His disciples (including us) was the Great Commission, a requirement for each of us who follows Him. "Go and make disciples of all nations," Jesus told us, "teaching them to obey everything I have commanded you" (Matthew 28:19,20).

Disciples must make other disciples. The disciplined, orderly followers (who by being disciplined and orderly followers become fruitful leaders) are to help others become disciplined, orderly followers, who in turn will become fruitful leaders, who will also help others become orderly followers. So the lineage of discipleship perpetuates itself.

Usually when we think of the Great Commission we think of missions, theological seminaries, Bible schools, churches, Sunday schools, parachurch organizations, and other ministries. But the Great Commission is first and foremost for every parent. Our mandate as parents is to disciple our children, to provide the disciplines of life which will help them become disciples of Jesus Christ, which will help them disciple their own children. Fulfilling this mandate is not a chore but a delight.

Looking back through the years, I believe my greatest delight was helping my children become Christ's disciples, then mature into discipling parents, fulfilling the Great Commission in their own families. I can't honestly say that I got up each morning and said, "I'm going to have fun doing some of this Great Commission stuff today." But Arlie and I plunged into the task of parenting and found it to be a true joy. The discipline of parenting, the discipline of helping to shape our children's lives for Christ, was much work, but transcending the work, it was a delight.

Discipling our children has mostly been through talking with our children. Sometimes it came through consciously talking to them about God. Most often, I believe, it came through the informal dialogues of daily living, casual conversations that arose naturally when we saw the majesty of a cloud and talked of its Maker, smelled a rose and spoke of His gifts, heard a house wren rival a great symphony and wondered together about God and His ways.

Is talking with my children a discipline for them? Yes, it's part of the task of guiding my children toward orderly living as disciples of Christ. Whether that talk is informal, spontaneous, or planned, it is talk that is in keeping with what Christ wants my children to be (and I want them to be what He wants them to be).

Talking with our children is a discipline for parents also. It is part of the plan to cultivate their lives in an orderly fashion. It is part of what we consciously or subconsciously have established as our goals for them.

"Here's the way to tie your shoes" doesn't sound much like the Great Commission. Neither does toilet training. But both disciplines are essential to discipleship, to orderly living on behalf of the Savior. Likewise, discipleship requires the most elementary talk that cultivates good etiquette, good eating habits, good sleeping habits, tasteful appearance, good grooming, habits of daily Bible reading, habits of daily prayer, and habits of daily conversations concerning the Lord. These kinds of talk are all part of the discipline for ordered lives, and ordered lives are necessary for the formation of a disciple.

Imagine a Christian leader who has matured through the disciplines of life to lead others in those disciplines, but is unable to tie his shoes, has slovenly etiquette, exemplifies poor habits of eating and sleeping, and is a model of poor appearance. Imagine a Christian leader who is ready to lead but who has not cultivated the habit of daily Bible reading, daily prayer, or daily conversations about the Lord.

The Great Commission for parents embraces some very ordinary talks about very ordinary things. But these become extraordinary matters when our children emerge to lead others. So we should delight to engage in these disciplines because we recognize their extraordinary value throughout our child's life. You may never have considered toilet training your child (and the necessary talks to make it happen) as part of the Great Commission, but it is. It's part of the orderly life of the disciple in order to become an effective Christian parent and leader.

My plea is for you to see even the most mundane part of parenting as part of the Great Commission, fitting your child to become Christ's disciple, and thus to disciple others. I've heard many of you young mothers bemoan the ordinary things you must do with your children daily, thinking at times that they are too ordinary to enjoy. But I would urge you to see these ordinary disciplines as part of the extraordinary task that Christ ordained you to do through the Great Commission. When you sense how very important these little talks and daily disciplines are, you will sense a delight in doing them, for you will see them as part of making disciples for Christ. And that, dear parent, is reason for us to delight in our task, even in the disciplines of daily talk and daily walk with our children.

In summary, here are some of the delights of discipline with our children:

1) Punishment is only one facet of discipline, that wide range of guidance that helps us move our children, or others, to learn leadership by learning to follow through orderly living.

2) Discipline becomes a delight when we anticipate the fruits that come from the discipline.

3) Discipline is that which we do to make disciples. For the Christian, the Great Commission is Christ's mandate for us to help others become His disciples.

4) Parenting is discipling. We are in the business of helping our children learn to become leaders by learning to be followers. Christian parenting is helping our children become Christ's disciples, who will in turn help others become Christ's disciples.

5) Helping our children become Christ's disciples can be one of the most delightful of all experiences as we anticipate the fruitful lives they can lead as His disciples.

6) Discipling our children is accomplished largely through our talk with them and our ordered role-modeling for them.

7) Discipling our children for Christ involves some very ordinary talk and activity, with some very extraordinary purposes and results.

19

Talking Without Words

I have two vivid memories of my preschool life. One is sitting on my mother's lap, listening to her read poetry. The other is sitting on my father's lap, listening to his big pocket watch and watching him play games with two little pieces of paper stuck to his fingers.

My parents were grain farmers with limited education. In the days when they grew up it was quite an achievement to finish high school. Most farm boys, and often girls, quit school to help their parents on the family farm. Compulsory education had not yet become law.

My preschool years came immediately after the Great Depression, which left its mark on Midwestern farmers. We had nothing—except each other.

I grew up by standards that would be called "deprived" or "poverty" today. We had no money to go places, so we stayed home and talked our evenings away on our front porch. We could not afford children's books, so my mother read to me from Longfellow, Lowell, Bryant, and a host of other poets she loved in her growing-up years. There were no such things as TV, stereos, VCR's, CD's, or computers, and even if we had had any of these, we had no electricity to operate them. In my preschool years we had no telephone, no toaster, no refrigerator, no freezer, no furnace, no air conditioner, no microwave oven, and none of dozens of other items considered essential in our modern homes today.

By today's standards we were poor, very poor. But in some ways I lived in utter luxury.

How many children growing up today can sit with their family throughout the evening, every evening, and talk? That is a lost luxury. How many children today have a mother or father who take them on their laps and read to them or play games with them as though time meant nothing? That too is a lost luxury. How many children growing up today can know for sure that the entire family will be at the table together for all three meals every day, seven days each week, 52 weeks each year, and will stay there together for the entire meal without jumping up to go somewhere? That is a lost luxury.

So while my poverty was painfully oppressive, it made these lost luxuries possible. Today much of the material luxury we offer our children carries with it personal and spiritual poverty. We enrich our children with *things* but impoverish them with our absence. We stuff our children with junk food but starve them for our affection. Our children have more spending money in the elementary ages than their grandparents had as adults, but by the time they grow up to be adults they will have had less family togetherness than their grandparents had as elementary-age children.

We provide our children with computer technology to gather unlimited information, but we won't take the time and effort to teach them the difference between right and wrong. We spend millions to educate our children in a values vacuum, but we gag at spending more than $9.95 for a Christian children's book that will help them learn Christian values. Most of all, we will give our children anything they ask for . . . except ourselves! Most children I know would trade in their material things for time with Mom or Dad, and would gladly have far less stuff in exchange for more hugs and kisses from their parents.

While growing up I enjoyed a wealth of words from parents and other family members who talked with me. Without TV we had only each other to talk with, so that's what we did. But as I think about it, I believe some of our greatest talk was wordless talk.

Was it Mom's poetry that offered warmth and presence? Partly. I loved to hear her read. She was so enthusiastic about these great poets. It seems a little incongruous now, but there she was, a postdepression farm lady with limited education, reading the great poets to her preschool son!

But I think there is a more significant reason why Mom's poetry is one of the two dominant memories of my preschool years. I sat on her lap while she read. I felt the warmth of her presence. I felt the tenderness of her embrace. The most professional reader in the world could not have competed with Mom, not even with a five-star TV production.

That's the same reason my other dominant preschool memory is sitting on Dad's lap. I felt the warmth of his presence. I heard his voice without electronics interfering with it.

In addition to the words that Mom and Dad spoke, there was a dialogue of personhood, the conversation of touch, the warmth of personal presence, the dynamic of their voice uncorrupted by devices. They were there! And I was the star of their little show at that moment. It wasn't much of a show by entertainment standards—a little kid in bib overalls sitting on the lap of a grain farmer with bib overalls (both with lots of patches)—but it was a magnificent performance by a little boy's standards. What child doesn't long to have Mother's or Father's full attention, uninterrupted and undiluted, with much tenderness thrown in? Some of you reading this would gladly have given up the material luxuries of your childhood for a loving embrace, a kiss on the cheek, and the sure knowledge that there was a lap on which you could crawl at any time and be lovingly received with no deadline as to when you had to get off.

Arlie and I have tried to give this same kind of dialogue of tenderness for our children. We were lavish with our affection. With five children and my chosen career, we didn't have much material abundance to shower on them, but we ourselves were there. I can't think of one of them who was deprived of words or wordless dialogue.

Our children are grown now, but during their growing-up years they were on my lap and Arlie's lap hundreds of times. Sometimes we read, sometimes we played games, sometimes we laughed, sometimes we talked. But the important thing is that we were there; the dialogue of touch was in operation. With words and wordless communications we said, "I love you and I am with you."

Now that my children are grown, I love to take my grandchildren on my lap, cuddle them, talk with them, hug them, sing to them cheek-to-cheek. The warmth of touch is security, the underpinnings of wholesome self-image. I would not need to say "I love you" when I hold one of my grandchildren. The warmth of presence says that without uttering a word. This is wordless talk.

A wide range of body language speaks without words. A smile is wordless warmth. Have you seen a friend's eyes twinkle when he or she talks with you? Do you know by a friend's posture if he is angry at you?

I would not want my children or grandchildren to grow up without my words. But I also would not want them to grow up without my smile, my touch, my hugs, my lap.

Would you?

In summary, here is some wordless communication with your children that you won't want to miss:

1) There is something secure about sitting on Mom's or Dad's lap—the security of personal presence. Your lap may not look like much to you, but to your young child it's a haven.

2) Don't forget to smile or let your eyes radiate your love. Twinkling eyes and a smiling face speak volumes.

3) A hug is affirmation, a statement that you are very important to me, personhood embracing personhood. Hugs don't cost you much, but they are priceless to your child.

4) A young child's self-image is enhanced by your touch, a kiss on the cheek, an embrace, the child's hand clasped tightly in yours, or your child's cheek next to your cheek while you sing softly.

20

Devotions: If Five Minutes Are Good, Is an Hour Better?

Do you remember the woman with a large wooden spoon who made her children sit through two-hour devotions? This misguided woman was so intense about devotions that she was force-feeding her children and trying to make them like it. "If five minutes are good for devotions, isn't an hour better?" was her creed. And why not two hours? She was serious, but woefully off-base. Her children will rebel, not only against the devotions, but against the Lord and His Word. They will grow up thinking that God is a stern disciplinarian who whacks them with wooden spoons to make them listen to Him and obey Him. These devotions will become counterproductive, defeating the very purpose they were meant to fulfill.

I have encountered a wide range of views concerning family devotions, or family altar, through the years. I've met the relaxed Christians who have no specific time for devotions with their children. Perhaps they don't have time. Or perhaps they don't take the time. It's a habit, you know, something that has to be established and maintained.

Other Christians I have met go to the opposite extreme—establishing family devotions and an unbending, unyielding, inflexible time, like the woman with the wooden spoon. "We are going to have this time together, and even if we have to whack people and enforce a rigid control over life, we will do it!"

In between, I've met Christian parents who represent a wide range of views and practice. Our own family fell into this category. We established a set time after dinner. But we recognized that there were times when the kids were under pressure to do something or get something done, and we made allowances for that. Devotions became a goal to achieve rather than a rigid rule to enforce. And there were times when we went away from formal devotions for awhile. But we always came back.

Looking back, I'm glad we always tried to make our time together fun. At first blush we might be tempted to think that the time for devotions is family worship, so we should enter into it with sober faces and hushed tones. In a sense that is true, because we are dealing with the Lord's business. But radiating the serious side of the Lord's business is the word "delight."

The Bible is filled with reminders that we should delight in the Lord. The psalmist said that the godly person's "delight is in the law of the Lord" (Psalm 1:2). I think this means we should enjoy God's Word, find joy in it. For a child this spells fun. The psalmist said also, "Delight yourself in the Lord and he will give you the desires of your heart" (Psalm 37:4). "I delight in your decrees; I will not neglect your word" (Psalm 119:16). "Your statutes are my delight; they are my counselors" (Psalm 119:24). "Direct me in the path of your commands, for there I find delight" (Psalm 119:35). "I delight in your commandments because I love them" (Psalm 119:47). "If your law had not been my delight, I would have perished in my affliction" (Psalm 119:92). "Trouble and distress have come upon me, but your commands are my delight" (Psalm 119:143). "I delight greatly in the Lord; my soul rejoices in my God" (Isaiah 61:10). "In my inner being I delight in God's law" (Romans 7:22).

Whatever else we do with our children, all our talks during devotions should point to the delights in the Lord and in His Word. One of my primary missions in life is to stir in my children a delight in God and His Word. To me that is a more significant mission than teaching them abundant principles or facts from the Word, even though I've tried to do that too. If I create in my children, and grandchildren, a delight in God's Word, they will form lifelong habits of reading and studying it. The principles and facts will come throughout their lifetimes.

Why do we have specific times with our children when we read His Word? I think there are many reasons, but let me share a few:

1) As Christians we should develop the habit of meeting God each day, enjoying what He has said and lingering in His presence. This is a small oasis in the desert of modern living, a safe harbor where we may retreat from the stormy seas of life, a refuge from the aggressive and destructive tendencies of modern society. We need this time each day to get to know God and to understand how we should live for Him.

2) Society today is not conducive to family togetherness. So much of modern living is designed to pull us apart rather than bring us together. Family devotions are a time of commitment that says we will be together. Your children may not seem enthusiastic about this time, but deep down they will grow to cherish a definite time when the family says, "We will be together!"

3) This book is about talking together as a family. But we must scramble to find specific times when we can talk. Family devotions establish a time for talking which says, "We will talk with each other now, about ourselves, our needs, our God, and His Word."

4) In the context of daily living we focus more on immediate or urgent matters. We seldom take time to reflect, to ponder, to meditate, to linger in God's presence, to worship. Family devotions can be a time to cultivate the joy of quietness, the delight of lingering or meditating in God's presence. The TV mentality violates our sense of meditation or reflection. It produces a world of hype and glitz, with lots of movement and action and fast words. We simply can't cultivate an internal peace with so much harangue. We need a time each day to meditate in God's Word and in His presence. Family devotions will help your child develop this special time.

5) Your child needs your guidance in God's Word, and what this means for daily living. Devotions become a time to mutually search the Word and talk about it together. Devotions are a special time when your child should seek your insights to help his own life.

6) Families that pray together stay together. Devotions become a time to cultivate family prayer. You learn to pray together, to pray for each other, and to enjoy prayer.

How long should family devotions be? I would rather keep them too short than too long because I'm sold on building the child's appetite for the Word rather than force-feeding the Word. You will have to decide your child's level of tolerance. You may want to start with five minutes each day. After a time, if devotions have become a time of delight, you could add a couple of minutes, even going up to ten. In my mind a half-hour is too long. Fifteen minutes is pushing it.

Remember, you are not trying to give your child a full Bible school education, but rather you are trying to build a special delight in God and His Word (and in family devotions!). Keep it short and keep it simple.

So what do we do during family devotions? Plan ahead with a variety of things. *Little Talks About God and You* and *More Little Talks About God and You* (Harvest House) are two books designed to give you a short five-minute talking time with your child. Each book has 100 little talks and each will take five to ten minutes, depending on how much talking your child and you do. But they are designed to stimulate talk between you and your child, talk that focuses on God's Word and God's truth.

The Muffin Family books (Harvest House) are also designed for family devotion time. There is a Bible story to read one day and a Muffin-correlating story to read the next day. There is application material which will help you talk about how the Muffin Family lives out Bible truth in their everyday lives.

Sometimes you may want to read a favorite Bible verse and talk about what it means in daily living. Or you may want to spend the five to ten minutes memorizing that verse. One of our favorite activities was Bible quiz time. After we had a certain number of Bible stories, we had quizzes to see what the children remembered.

One day you may want to talk about some hurts your child is feeling. How does God respond to these hurts? Or perhaps some hurts a friend is feeling. How does God respond to these? Your child may have some special delight. Spend the five minutes talking about that delight and how pleased God is about it. Close the time with a short prayer thanking God for this special delight.

Is there a friend who needs prayer? Take one five-minute devotion to talk about how God wants to help that friend, and then pray a short prayer, or ask your child to pray a short prayer, for this friend.

Help your child discover the joy of prayer. To many Christians prayer sounds dull, and that shouldn't be the case. Practice short prayers. Help your child focus each time on one type of prayer:

1) Intercession—when your child asks God's help for another person.

2) Petition—when your child asks God's help for his own needs.

3) Confession—when your child talks with God about something he has done wrong, and asks God to forgive him and help him stay away from such things.

4) Praise—when we tell God how good He is, and how glad we are that we can be His children and do what He wants us to. Praise focuses on God and how we delight in Him.

5) Thanksgiving—when we thank God for food, or clothing, or something special He has helped your child get, or for each other in the family, or for your home. Make a list of things for which you and your child are thankful. Pray for one each day.

When should you have family devotions? Not at a point in the day when life is on the fast track. Don't put this time just before your child has to rush off to school unless you allow extra time after breakfast, and don't mix the rush of the day with the delight of lingering in God's presence. We liked to do this after dinner. Or you may prefer to do it just before the child's bedtime. The time is less important than doing it with reasonable regularity and doing it with delight.

Family devotions is a time of golden opportunity for you to talk with your child. Somewhere in our busy days we must have five minutes we can give to this very important activity. It's a question of priorities, isn't it?

In summary, here are some important guidelines for your family devotions:

1) Set apart one special time each day for family devotions, and stick with it. Make this a habit or it will fall by the wayside. But don't make it so rigid that you can't miss one occasionally when it would create family pressure to enforce the devotions.

2) Make your time together a time of delight. Don't make devotions too serious all the time, but mix the serious and the fun together so that your child will want to come back next time.

3) Keep family devotions short. Start with five minutes. Rarely go over 15 minutes. Keep the word "delight" always before you. It is hard for a young child to be delighted in long devotions.

4) Vary the menu from a list of basics. Do different things, but let these be things from a set list. Basically you are focusing on daily living, God's Word for daily living, learning to pray, and learning about God.

5) Be sure to focus devotions on talking together. If you read from a book, talk about what you have read. If you are going to pray for someone, talk about this person and his need, and how God may want to help him.

6) Occasionally talk with your child about the time you are spending together. What does he like best? Are there other things he would like to do? But sometimes you need to do what you know is best. Your child may not appear to enjoy everything now, but we have found years later that our children did enjoy things that did not seem so enjoyable at the time.

21

Five Great Things TV Can't Do for Your Children

Not long ago three of our grandchildren stayed overnight with us. We like to do this from time to time to help us spend more quality time with each of them. But late in the day I felt the pressure to get some work done, too. My first instinct was to put a videotape in the VCR and plop the grandchildren in front of the tube.

You know the feeling, don't you? How many times this last week have you turned to the TV as an electronic babysitter? How many times have you breathed a sigh of relief when the kids want to watch TV, thereby giving you some down time?

Sometimes that's okay, but too often we begin to lean heavily on the tube to babysit. Where is the boundary between enough and too much? I can't answer that question for you. You must judge for yourself and your family. But we both know there are dangerous boundaries where TV becomes a surrogate parent.

Consider some statistics. More homes in America (98 percent) have TV sets than indoor toilets. The typical middle-class American has at least three TV sets. The typical American spends 2300 hours each year watching TV compared to 2000 hours each year earning a living (40 hours per week times 50 weeks). The average American child watches TV an average of six hours per day, as much time as he spends in school. By the time a child enters kindergarten, he has watched as much as 8000 hours of TV.

To put it bluntly, TV-watching equals or exceeds breadwinning for adults and education for children. Put this in perspective with the time we spend in church, Sunday school, Christian activities, family devotions, or personal Bible study and we easily become embarrassed. Who among us spends much more than four to five hours weekly on all these combined unless we are in career ministry?

Several years ago an important survey was conducted among evangelicals and fundamentalists to determine TV-watching habits. The survey concluded that the evangelical-fundamentalist population had essentially the same TV-watching habits as society at large. If Mom and Dad are like everyone else in their TV habits, why should they complain if their children are like everyone else in their TV habits? With our children, our role-modeling will always win over our sermonizing.

So why should I care if my children watch TV the way their school friends do? Doesn't that free me to do my thing more?

First, consider those 2000 hours each year that your child "invests" in the tube. Is this the best use of 2000 hours? If your child spends that many hours with the tube, what's left for 1) family talk together, 2) family devotions, 3) good reading, 4) playtime, 5) creative development through good activities, and 6) quiet time, a time to grow without hype and glitz?

Second, are you *sure* you know what your child is watching? While the tube is babysitting, it is also indoctrinating. It is teaching your child some severely distorted values. Almost everything you believe as a Christian is at times ridiculed or belittled or made to look unimportant on TV. Occasionally we see wholesome values emerge, but this has become the exception rather than the rule. We grow accustomed to the distorted idea that wrong is really okay after all.

Third, anytime you turn your parental task over to a group of high-powered strangers, you can expect them to do it their way. I really don't want a ratings-hungry producer raising my children or grandchildren.

Fourth, would you really want to raise your child by the lifestyle standards portrayed on the tube? Would you really want your child involved daily in real-life gore, violence, sex, coarse language, distorted family images, values vacuum, and anti-Christian thinking?

You and I would not think of exposing our children to all these things in real life. But we carelessly involve our children in a projection of these things into a bigger-than-life impact.

Fifth, contrast the pace on TV with the pace you desire in your family living. To paraphrase an old song title, "How do you keep them on the farm after they've watched TV?" We talked in the last chapter about our urgent needs, as children and adults, for quiet times, times to reflect or meditate about God, times to "smell the flowers," time to be creative, time to meet God. Your child cannot do any of these things while the tube is blasting at him full-tilt. Neither can you.

Sixth, are you satisfied with the typical TV character as a role model for your children? What if your child became this type of person? Would you be satisfied? Or do you have a different goal for your child?

It's easy to think that TV has so much hype and glitz that we parents can never compete with it: Our kids are hooked, so we may as well give up. That is a myth; it simply is not true. Your children are hungry for you as a person. TV can't even begin to compete with you if you are willing to personally involve yourself with your children and talk with them.

Here are five things that TV can't do for your child. But you can do each of them.

1) TV can't speak your child's name (or yours) unless generically by accident. TV has absolutely no personal interest in your child and does not even know that he exists. If he died, TV would not shed one tear. Your child is a nonperson, a mere statistic, nothing more than one more unit in the total audience profile. TV is totally disinterested in who your child is, what he thinks, how she acts, what he learned in school today, whether she loves God or hates Him, and whether he loves you or hates you. Other than a marketing-profile statistic, TV has no personal concern for your child whatsoever.

But you, dear parent, have the opportunity—no, the privilege—of whispering your child's name to her a hundred times each day. And with it you can transmit vibes that no TV set can send out, vibes of personal concern and interest that your child is sure to pick up.

2) TV can't cuddle up with your child on its lap and read a book to him. TV has no lap, like my mother and father had, like Arlie and I have had, like you have, on which to hold the child. TV is not interested in flesh-and-blood contact, in touch, in personal warmth. There is no warm breath, no sound of a mother's heart beating, no twinkling eyes looking into my child's face, no sweet smile directed at that one VIP sitting on my lap, no one-on-one personal communications.

What TV said to your child this morning was not really said to your child. It was directed to a marketing image out there. Your child was included only as a statistic, not as a person with personal needs. What you said to your child this morning came from a heart of loving concern, a desire for that individual's success, a yearning for that one person to come to know God.

TV will never replace listening to a good book while sitting on a parent's lap unless we parents abdicate our royal rights and privileges and turn them over to strangers with a radically different agenda from ours.

3) TV will never hug your child when she cuts her finger or his friends make fun of him. At that moment of personal hurt and personal need, your child can never rush into the room, turn on the tube, and get the solace he needs. It's not there!

But *you* are there. It's your warm hug that counts at a time like that. All the five-star productions in New York are worthless at a moment like that. But a simple, yet loving, hug from Mom or Dad is everything.

Remember the power you possess in a hug. All the electronics in the world can never compete with a parent's loving hug, a tender embrace for a hurting little person. We adults need that too. We would gladly trade vast resources for a genuine hug from a caring person when life hits the fan.

TV will never replace a hug because it has no heart to care for your hurting child. Actually the tube has no brain to recognize your child's hurts. And it certainly has no arms to embrace him.

4) TV can never listen to your child. Among the many gifts a child wants from his parents is a listening ear. But TV has no ear. It cannot and will not listen when she rushes in the door and is excited about a new part in the school play. It cannot and will not listen when he wants to tell you about a new friend at school or getting on the Little League team. TV will

ignore your child when she wants to ask the simple question "Do you still love me?"

TV reminds me of a storm sewer I watched following a thunderstorm. From somewhere the pipeline is filled and just keeps on flowing out, whether we like it or not. You can never send anything back through the pipeline; it's all one way. TV spills out its words and images, and if you're there, you get dumped on. But try asking it one simple question. Try telling it what's on your heart. It has no ears to hear, no heart to care if it could hear. You are a nobody and your child is a nobody—just another statistical ear on which it can dump its one-way stream.

But you have a wonderful privilege when your child bursts through the door with exciting news: You can listen! At that moment you are more important to your child than all the TV sets in the world—if you truly listen! More than anything else at that moment, your child wants a listening ear with a direct connection to a caring heart.

TV can never replace a listening parent. It will never do that unless you relinquish your role as a listening parent! Then where else can your child turn but to the unsympathetic box with its steady barrage of uncaring words? And if we parents don't listen, how can we convince our child that God does?

5) TV can never tuck your child in bed at night and pray with him. Never! But you can. You have a one-in-a-million opportunity to do a simple act of love that all the TV producers in the world can't send out through those little boxes.

TV can't talk with your child about the good things and the not-so-good things that happened to her today. It will not put a soft hand on his brow and ask how he feels. It will not put a thermometer in her mouth and get a drink of water for her. It will not take hold of your child's hand gently and say "I love you." TV will never kiss your child goodnight.

In case you don't know, you are the star of the show. TV can never compete with what you have to offer your child. You will far outshine TV in your child's eyes, unless you turn your parenting over to the tube.

In summary, here are five great things TV cannot do for your child, but you can:

1) You can speak your child's name, lovingly and often, caring deeply for your child as a person, a unique individual. TV can't do that.

2) You can cuddle up with your child on your lap and read a good book to him. You can smile, look into your child's eyes, and hold her hand. No TV set in the world can do that.

3) You can hug your child when she cuts her finger or friends make fun of him, imparting a personal consolation that says "I love you." TV can never do that.

4) You can listen to your child with a ready ear and a caring heart. When your child needs someone to talk with, you can be there to listen. No TV set in the world will ever listen to your child.

5) You can tuck your child in bed at night and talk about his concerns and interests, pray with him, talk with her about God. TV can never do that.

22

Your Child Is Listening...
But Who Is Talking?

We're drowning in words, but we're dying of thirst for meaning. Everywhere we turn, someone is talking to us. The average American listens to at least 2000 hours of TV each year. By the time a child is 18 and ready for college, he has listened to 36,000 hours of TV. Multiply that times the number of words that TV spits out in an hour. Every year millions of words are dumped on us by TV.

Add to that the books we read, as well as the newspapers, magazines, and conversations—and suddenly we realize we are awash in words. We do not lack at all for words; what we lack is *meaning*.

We don't truly listen to all the words we hear. Hearing and listening are vastly different, just as words and meaning are vastly different. We hear words, but we listen to meaning.

If I casually hear a TV character say to another, "I love you," it doesn't mean much to me. What do I care if two fictitious strangers talk of love, especially if I know it's only a drama hatched up by a producer and his team? But if I have become personally involved (vicariously, of course) with the drama, those words have a little more meaning to me.

When Arlie, or one of my children or grandchildren, says "I love you," the same three words take on deep meaning. That's because the person who spoke them is a very significant person to me.

An unsavory character passes you on the street, leers at you, and says "I love you." You are repulsed. Your child or grandchild climbs on your lap and whispers "I love you." You are delighted. Same words, different meaning. When people who are significant to you say something, what they say becomes more significant because they are significant.

I often wondered why young people gravitate to cults until I interviewed two experts on cults. "Why?" I asked them. "Is it because some special cult doctrine appeals to the new convert?"

"Joining a cult has nothing to do with doctrine," both agreed. Then they explained. At home, parents forgot to put their arms around their growing child. They neglected to say, "I love you. I appreciate you." Then a member of a cult came along. For the first time someone said, "I love you. I appreciate you." The young person, starving for affection and attention, was willing to join a cult to get what he thought would be true love.

This is where life gets very confusing for such a young person. The person who meant the most to him, his parent, never spoke the words that meant the most: "I love you." But someone who meant the least to him spoke the words that meant the most.

Kids join cults because parents don't talk with their kids. Parents forget to say "I love you." A child wants to hear those words most from parents because parents mean the most to the child. But if parents abdicate their role, and a cult member assumes it, the young person will shift to a meaningless person to get the meaningful message he wanted so much from his parent.

Parents, if you don't talk with your children, if you don't establish a meaningful relationship with them through your talk, someone else will. If you don't develop a strong bond with your child through conversation, or dialogue, someone else will. And you may not like the unsavory characters who say "I love you" to your child and find a listening ear.

Your child *will* listen to someone. He wants most of all to listen to you, talk with you, come to love you, let you guide him. But if you refuse, he will listen to someone else. Your child searches for meaning in life and expects to find it first in you. But if your priorities don't give you the time to communicate meaning, someone else will come along. A few meaningful words such as "I love you" by such a person may sidetrack your child into an incredible amount of meaningless follow-up, such as cult doctrine or peer pressure.

Arlie and I have been parents for 35 years. That represents a lot of parenting. There were times when we wondered if we were putting too much of our time in parenting. What about our own interests? Were we not entitled to "do our own thing"? Perhaps, but with five children, we decided to focus on each other and our children.

Our children are grown now. We're all very close. We love to spend time together, we love to do things together, we enjoy eating or hiking or talking together. Perhaps that's because we have always done these things together.

Now that our children are grown and have become our best friends, we're glad for every moment we spent with them. Now that our children have all become

Christians and married Christians and purpose to raise their families as Christians, we realize that we gave up so little to be rewarded so richly.

My plea to you who are parents of young children is to invest your prime time with them. I wish you could know now what joy will come to you through the years if you make your family your primary focus.

If you come into our home when our children are here you will find us talking. An occasional good program on TV is okay, like watching the Chicago Cubs or the Bears. But when Ron and Brad and I watch, we laugh and talk about the plays, critique a ridiculous commercial, or talk of other things as we watch. But mostly we like to talk. That's because we have always talked together as a family.

If I could give you one gift through this book, it would be the desire to talk with your children. As parents who have been talking with their children all these years, we urge you to start now. Don't let another day go by before you begin to cultivate this most wonderful habit with the VIP's of your life, your children.

In summary, my plea for you is:

1) Recognize that your children and spouse are the most important people in your life other than God Himself. They, and you, seek meaning from each other. But if you don't impart meaning to your children through your talking, they will seek it elsewhere and may listen to unsavory characters who impart transient meaning, but with long-lasting harm.

2) Your children want to talk with you and listen to you because you are the most significant person in the world to them. They trust you to fulfill your role as parent, imparting meaning through conversation, and if you don't, they will listen to someone else.

3) Begin today, without waiting, to cultivate a talking relationship with your children. No child is too young, or too old, to talk with him.

4) Ask God to help you cultivate the most wonderful relationship with your children through talking with them. He will!

Other Good
Harvest House Reading

LITTLE TALKS ABOUT GOD AND YOU
by *V. Gilbert Beers*

If you're wondering what to do for family devotions, now is
the time to stop wondering and start reading *Little Talks About
God and You*. Illustrated on every page, each little talk includes
a small story to illustrate a Bible truth, questions to share with
your child, a Bible reading, and a prayer. These little talks will
lead you and your child through a refreshing, fun-filled
exploration of life. Gil Beers, past editor of *Christianity Today*, is
well known for his children's literature. Illustrated.

MORE LITTLE TALKS ABOUT GOD AND YOU
by *V. Gilbert Beers*

Popular children's author Gilbert Beers has done it again in
this memorable sequel. If you had five or ten minutes to spend
with your child tonight, what would you do? By sharing one
of these "little talks" with your child each day, you'll be
building your child's character and his/her relationship with
God and you. The 100 little talks each include a Bible reading,
a Bible truth, and a prayer and help you nurture a lifelong
relationship with your child. Perfect for ages 3-8.

THE MUFFIN FAMILY SERIES
by *V. Gilbert Beers*

Harvest House is pleased to reintroduce the well-known
Muffin Family! The first of twelve 96-page, full-color Muffin
books to be released under the *Growing Up with God* series
logo, each book has been completely redesigned by ever-
popular children's author Gil Beers. Each book features several
story couplets: a Bible story with a special Bible truth about the
way a Bible-time person lived for God, and a Muffin Family
story with that same Bible truth at work in a family much like
yours. After each story couplet, an application section has
been added to help parent and child apply what they have
learned to daily living. These *Growing Up with God* books will
help parents encourage important values in their children such
as honesty, truthfulness, and patience. Ages 4 to 12.

> **GROWING UP WITH JESUS**
> **GROWING UP WITH MY FAMILY**
> **GROWING UP TO PRAISE GOD**
> **GROWING UP WITH GOD'S FRIENDS**

Dear Reader:

We would appreciate hearing from you regarding this Harvest House nonfiction book. It will enable us to continue to give you the best in Christian publishing.

1. What most influenced you to purchase *Parents, Talk With Your Children*?
   - ☐ Author
   - ☐ Subject matter
   - ☐ Backcover copy
   - ☐ Recommendations
   - ☐ Cover/Title
   - ☐ _____

2. Where did you purchase this book?
   - ☐ Christian bookstore
   - ☐ General bookstore
   - ☐ Department store
   - ☐ Grocery store
   - ☐ Other

3. Your overall rating of this book:
   ☐ Excellent ☐ Very good ☐ Good ☐ Fair ☐ Poor

4. How likely would you be to purchase other books by this author?
   - ☐ Very likely
   - ☐ Somewhat likely
   - ☐ Not very likely
   - ☐ Not at all

5. What types of books most interest you? (check all that apply)
   - ☐ Women's Books
   - ☐ Marriage Books
   - ☐ Current Issues
   - ☐ Self Help/Psychology
   - ☐ Bible Studies
   - ☐ Fiction
   - ☐ Biographies
   - ☐ Children's Books
   - ☐ Youth Books
   - ☐ Other _____

6. Please check the box next to your age group.
   - ☐ Under 18
   - ☐ 18-24
   - ☐ 25-34
   - ☐ 35-44
   - ☐ 45-54
   - ☐ 55 and over

Mail to: Editorial Director
Harvest House Publishers
1075 Arrowsmith
Eugene, OR 97402

Name _____

Address _____

City _____ State _____ Zip _____

Thank you for helping us to help you in future publications!